A gift for:

_____

The Lord will guide you always; he will satisfy your needs in a sun-scorched land and will strengthen your frame. You will be like a well-watered garden, like a spring whose waters never fail.

ISAIAH 58:11

From:

_____

Requests for information should be addressed to:
Inspirio, the gift group of Zondervan
Grand Rapids, Michigan 49530
www.inspiriogifts.com

Compilers: Patricia Lutherbeck and Betsy Williams
in association with Snapdragon Editorial Group
Project Manager: Tom Dean
Production Management: Matt Nolan
Design: Michael J. Williams

Printed in the United States of America
10 9 8 7 / 10 9 8 7 6 5

Daily Promises for
Women of Color

from the
New International Version

inspirio™

Contents

God's promises are like the stars; the darker the night the brighter they shine.

—David Nicholas

Introduction

The great and glorious promises of God—they are our security in a world of uncertainty and turmoil. They are life vests, intended to protect us as we navigate stormy seas. They are God's gifts given corporately to all of his children—but personally to each one of us.

We've compiled this book, *Daily Promises for Women of Color*, so that you can more easily take hold of God's promises for your life. We pray that as you read, you will begin to understand how vast his promises really are, covering virtually every area of daily life. Then, it's our hope that you will appropriate them as God intended, whether your skies are sunny or gray, in good times and bad. God's promises are sufficient to cover any need you might have.

So, read them, believe them, rely on them, and treasure them. Most of all, thank God for them. Though freely given, they have been bought with a great price—the holy, righteous blood of God's precious son, Jesus.

Bible

Oh, how I love your law!
I meditate on it all day long.
Your commands make me wiser than my enemies,
for they are ever with me, [O Lord].

PSALM 119:97–98

Jesus answered, "It is written: 'People do not live on bread alone, but on every word that comes from the mouth of God.'"

MATTHEW 4:4 TNIV

Your word is a lamp to my feet
and a light for my path.

PSALM 119:105

Jesus said, "The seed on good soil stands for those with a noble and good heart, who hear the word, retain it, and by persevering produce a crop."

LUKE 8:15

Jesus said, "Heaven and earth will pass away, but my words will never pass away."

MARK 13:31

Bible

If you pay attention to these laws and are careful to
follow them, then the LORD your God will keep his
covenant of love with you, as he swore to
your forefathers.

DEUTERONOMY 7:12

The law of the LORD is perfect,
reviving the soul.
The statutes of the LORD are trustworthy,
making wise the simple.

PSALM 19:7

Like newborn babies, crave pure spiritual milk, so
that by it you may grow up in your salvation.

1 PETER 2:2

When your words came, I ate them;
they were my joy and my heart's delight.

JEREMIAH 15:16

Great peace have they who love your law,
and nothing can make them stumble.

PSALM 119:165

Bible

Jesus replied, "Blessed ... are those who hear the word of God and obey it."

LUKE 11:28

All Scripture is God-breathed and is useful for teaching, rebuking, correcting and training in righteousness, so that all God's people may be thoroughly equipped for every good work.

2 TIMOTHY 3:16–17 TNIV

I remember your ancient laws, O LORD,
and I find comfort in them.

PSALM 119:52

Everything that was written in the past was written to teach us, so that through endurance and the encouragement of the Scriptures we might have hope.

ROMANS 15:4

The LORD said, "Do not let this Book of the Law depart from your mouth; meditate on it day and night, so that you may be careful to do everything written in it. Then you will be prosperous and successful."

JOSHUA 1:8

Bible

The word of God is living and active. Sharper than any double-edged sword, it penetrates even to dividing soul and spirit, joints and marrow; it judges the thoughts and attitudes of the heart.

HEBREWS 4:12

We have the word of the prophets made more certain, and you will do well to pay attention to it, as to a light shining in a dark place, until the day dawns and the morning star rises in your hearts.

2 PETER 1:19

Jesus said, "Others, like seed sown on good soil, hear the word, accept it, and produce a crop—thirty, sixty or even a hundred times what was sown."

MARK 4:20

"All people are like grass,
     and all their glory is like the flowers of the field;
the grass withers and the flowers fall,
     but the word of the Lord endures forever."

1 PETER 1:24–25 TNIV

Bible

I meditate on your precepts
  and consider your ways.
I delight in your decrees;
  I will not neglect your word.

PSALM 119:15–16

Do your best to present yourself to God as one approved, a workman who does not need to be ashamed and who correctly handles the word of truth.

2 TIMOTHY 2:15

Those who look intently into the perfect law that gives freedom and continue in it—not forgetting what they have heard but doing it—they will be blessed in what they do.

JAMES 1:25 TNIV

I have hidden your word in my heart
  that I might not sin against you.

PSALM 119:11

Blessed is the one who reads the words of this prophecy, and blessed are those who hear it and take to heart what is written in it, because the time is near.

REVELATION 1:3

Bible

Your statutes are wonderful;
*   therefore I obey them.*
The unfolding of your words gives light;
*   it gives understanding to the simple.*

PSALM 119:129–130

Let the word of Christ dwell in you richly as you
teach and admonish one another with all wisdom,
and as you sing psalms, hymns and spiritual songs
with gratitude in your hearts to God.

COLOSSIANS 3:16

In the beginning was the Word, and the Word was
with God, and the Word was God. He was with God
in the beginning.

JOHN 1:1–2

Your hands made me and formed me;
*   give me understanding to learn your commands.*
May those who fear you rejoice when they see me,
*   for I have put my hope in your word.*

PSALM 119:73–74

Blessings

Blessed are those
     who do not walk in step with the wicked
or stand in the way that sinners take
     or sit in the company of mockers,
but who delight in the law of the LORD
     and meditate on his law day and night.
They are like a tree planted by streams of water,
     which yields its fruit in season
and whose leaf does not wither—
     whatever they do prospers.

                                        PSALM 1:1–3 TNIV

The LORD your God will bless you in all your harvest and in all the work of your hands, and your joy will be complete.

                                        DEUTERONOMY 16:15

This is what the LORD says: ...

"Blessed are those who trust in the LORD,
     whose confidence is in him."

                                        JEREMIAH 17:5, 7 TNIV

Blessings

All these blessings will come upon you and accompany you if you obey the LORD your God:
You will be blessed in the city and blessed in the country.
The fruit of your womb will be blessed, and the crops of your land and the young of your livestock—the calves of your herds and the lambs of your flocks.
Your basket and your kneading trough will be blessed.
You will be blessed when you come in and blessed when you go out.
The LORD will send a blessing on your barns and on everything you put your hand to. The LORD your God will bless you in the land he is giving you.
The LORD will grant you abundant prosperity....
The LORD will open the heavens, the storehouse of his bounty, to send rain on your land in season and to bless all the work of your hands. You will lend to many nations but will borrow from none. The LORD will make you the head, not the tail.... You will always be at the top, never at the bottom.

DEUTERONOMY 28:2–6, 8, 11–13

Blessings

You have made known to me the path of life;
you will fill me with joy in your presence,
with eternal pleasures at your right hand.

PSALM 16:11

"I will satisfy the priests with abundance,
and my people will be filled with my bounty,"
declares the LORD.

JEREMIAH 31:14

Blessed are those you choose
and bring near to live in your courts!
We are filled with the good things of your house,
of your holy temple.

PSALM 65:4

Praise the LORD, O my soul,
and forget not all his benefits —
who satisfies your desires with good things
so that your youth is renewed like the eagle's.

PSALM 103:2, 5

Blessings

"Bring the whole tithe into the storehouse, that there may be food in my house. Test me in this," says the LORD Almighty, "and see if I will not throw open the floodgates of heaven and pour out so much blessing that you will not have room enough for it."

MALACHI 3:10

"I will make you into a great nation
and I will bless you;
I will make your name great,
and you will be a blessing.
I will bless those who bless you,
and whoever curses you I will curse;
and all peoples on earth
will be blessed through you," says the LORD.

GENESIS 12:2–3

From the fullness of his grace we have all received one blessing after another.

JOHN 1:16

God will meet all your needs according to his glorious riches in Christ Jesus.

PHILIPPIANS 4:19

Blessings

You care for the land and water it;
    you enrich it abundantly.
The streams of God are filled with water
    to provide the people with grain,
    for so you have ordained it.
You drench its furrows
    and level its ridges;
you soften it with showers
    and bless its crops.
You crown the year with your bounty,
    and your carts overflow with abundance.

PSALM 65:9–11

Every good and perfect gift is from above, coming
down from the Father of the heavenly lights, who
does not change like shifting shadows.

JAMES 1:17

Surely, O LORD, you bless the righteous;
    you surround them with your favor as with
a shield.

PSALM 5:12

Blessings

Jesus said, "The thief comes only to steal and kill and destroy; I have come that they may have life, and have it to the full."

JOHN 10:10

How priceless is your unfailing love, O God!
People take refuge in the shadow of your wings.
They feast on the abundance of your house;
you give them drink from your river of delights.

PSALM 36:7–8 TNIV

You gave abundant showers, O God;
you refreshed your weary inheritance.

PSALM 68:9

Now to him who is able to do immeasurably more than all we ask or imagine, according to his power that is at work within us, to him be glory in the church and in Christ Jesus throughout all generations, for ever and ever! Amen.

EPHESIANS 3:20–21

Character

The LORD does not look at the things human beings
look at. People look at the outward appearance, but
the LORD looks at the heart.

1 SAMUEL 16:7 TNIV

Jesus said,
*"Blessed are those who hunger and thirst for
    righteousness,
    for they will be filled."*

MATTHEW 5:6

*Your ways are in full view of the LORD,
    and he examines all your paths.*

PROVERBS 5:21 TNIV

We know that suffering produces perseverance;
perseverance, character; and character, hope. And
hope does not disappoint us, because God has
poured out his love into our hearts by the Holy
Spirit, whom he has given us.

ROMANS 5:3–5

*The highway of the upright avoids evil;
    those who guard their ways preserve their lives.*

PROVERBS 16:17 TNIV

Character

Jesus said, "I have set you an example that you should do as I have done for you."

JOHN 13:15

Blessed are they whose ways are blameless,
who walk according to the law of the LORD.

PSALM 119:1

Jesus said,
"Blessed are the merciful,
for they will be shown mercy."

MATTHEW 5:7

The noble make noble plans,
and by noble deeds they stand.

ISAIAH 32:8 TNIV

A good name is more desirable than great riches;
to be esteemed is better than silver or gold.

PROVERBS 22:1

Character

Listen ... to a father's instruction;
*   pay attention and gain understanding.*

PROVERBS 4:1

To this you were called, because Christ suffered for you, leaving you an example, that you should follow in his steps.

1 PETER 2:21

Be imitators of God, therefore, as dearly loved children and live a life of love, just as Christ loved us and gave himself up for us as a fragrant offering and sacrifice to God.

EPHESIANS 5:1–2

Jesus said, "Whoever wants to become great among you must be your servant, and whoever wants to be first must be slave of all."

MARK 10:43–44

This is how we know what love is: Jesus Christ laid down his life for us. And we ought to lay down our lives for one another.

1 JOHN 3:16 TNIV

Character

Dear children, let us not love with words or tongue but with actions and in truth.

1 JOHN 3:18

Don't let anyone look down on you because you are young, but set an example for the believers in speech, in life, in love, in faith and in purity.

1 TIMOTHY 4:12

Better the poor whose walk is blameless
than the rich whose ways are perverse.

PROVERBS 28:6 TNIV

In everything set them an example by doing what is good. In your teaching show integrity, seriousness and soundness of speech that cannot be condemned, so that those who oppose you may be ashamed because they have nothing bad to say about us.

TITUS 2:7–8

Be shepherds of God's flock that is under your care, serving as overseers—not because you must, but because you are willing, as God wants you to be; not greedy for money, but eager to serve; not lording it over those entrusted to you, but being examples to the flock.

1 PETER 5:2–3

Character

Who may ascend the mountain of the LORD?
  Who may stand in his holy place?
Those who have clean hands and a pure heart,
  who do not put their trust in an idol
or swear by a false god.

PSALM 24:3–4 TNIV

He has shown all you people what is good.
  And what does the LORD require of you?
To act justly and to love mercy
  and to walk humbly with your God.

MICAH 6:8 TNIV

This is what the LORD says:

"Stand at the crossroads and look;
  ask for the ancient paths,
ask where the good way is, and walk in it,
  and you will find rest for your souls."

JEREMIAH 6:16

Character

A wife of noble character who can find?
    She is worth far more than rubies.
She opens her arms to the poor
    and extends her hands to the needy.
She is clothed with strength and dignity;
    she can laugh at the days to come.
She speaks with wisdom,
    and faithful instruction is on her tongue.
Charm is deceptive, and beauty is fleeting;
    but a woman who fears the LORD is to be praised.

PROVERBS 31:10, 20, 25–26, 30

Do not merely listen to the word, and so deceive
yourselves. Do what it says. Those who listen to the
word but do not do what it says are like people who
look at their faces in a mirror and, after looking at
themselves, go away and immediately forget what
they look like. But those who look intently into
the perfect law that gives freedom and continue in
it — not forgetting what they have heard but
doing it — they will be blessed in what they do.

JAMES 1:22–25 TNIV

Church

You are a chosen people, a royal priesthood, a holy nation, a people belonging to God, that you may declare the praises of him who called you out of darkness into his wonderful light.

1 PETER 2:9

The body is a unit, though it is made up of many parts; and though all its parts are many, they form one body. So it is with Christ. For we were all baptized by one Spirit into one body — whether Jews or Greeks, slave or free — and we were all given the one Spirit to drink.

1 CORINTHIANS 12:12–13

God's household ... is the church of the living God, the pillar and foundation of the truth.

1 TIMOTHY 3:15

If we walk in the light, as he is in the light, we have fellowship with one another, and the blood of Jesus, his Son, purifies us from all sin.

1 JOHN 1:7

Church

[Christ] is the head of the body, the church; he is the beginning and the firstborn from among the dead, so that in everything he might have the supremacy.

COLOSSIANS 1:18

You are the body of Christ, and each one of you is a part of it. And in the church God has appointed first of all apostles, second prophets, third teachers, then workers of miracles, also those having gifts of healing, those able to help others, those with gifts of administration, and those speaking in different kinds of tongues.

1 CORINTHIANS 12:27–28

Let us not give up meeting together, as some are in the habit of doing, but let us encourage one another—and all the more as you see the Day approaching.

HEBREWS 10:25

Church

Since you are eager to have spiritual gifts, try to excel in gifts that build up the church.

1 CORINTHIANS 14:12

[God's] intent was that now, through the church, the manifold wisdom of God should be made known to the rulers and authorities in the heavenly realms.

EPHESIANS 3:10

Jesus replied, "Blessed are you, Simon son of Jonah, for this was not revealed to you by flesh and blood, but by my Father in heaven. And I tell you that you are Peter, and on this rock I will build my church, and the gates of death will not overcome it."

MATTHEW 16:17–18 TNIV

Christ loved the church and gave himself up for her to make her holy, cleansing her by the washing with water through the word, and to present her to himself as a radiant church, without stain or wrinkle or any other blemish, but holy and blameless.

EPHESIANS 5:25–27

Church

Just as each of us has one body with many members, and these members do not all have the same function, so in Christ we, though many, form one body, and each member belongs to all the others. We have different gifts, according to the grace given to each of us. If your gift is prophesying, then prophesy in accordance with your faith.

ROMANS 12:4–6 TNIV

Jesus said, "Where two or three come together in my name, there am I with them."

MATTHEW 18:20

You are no longer foreigners and aliens, but fellow citizens with God's people and members of God's household, built on the foundation of the apostles and prophets, with Christ Jesus himself as the chief cornerstone. In him the whole building is joined together and rises to become a holy temple in the Lord.

EPHESIANS 2:19–21

Church

How good and pleasant it is
*   when God's people live together in unity!*
It is like precious oil poured on the head,
*   running down on the beard,*
running down on Aaron's beard,
*   down on the collar of his robe.*
It is as if the dew of Hermon
*   were falling on Mount Zion.*
For there the LORD bestows his blessing,
*   even life forevermore.*

PSALM 133:1–3 TNIV

Let the word of Christ dwell in you richly as you teach and admonish one another with all wisdom, and as you sing psalms, hymns and spiritual songs with gratitude in your hearts to God.

COLOSSIANS 3:16

The elders who direct the affairs of the church well are worthy of double honor, especially those whose work is preaching and teaching.

1 TIMOTHY 5:17

Church

We have different gifts, according to the grace given to each of us. If your gift is prophesying, then prophesy in accordance with your faith; if it is serving, then serve; if it is teaching, then teach; if it is to encourage, then give encouragement; if it is giving, then give generously; if it is to lead, do it diligently; if it is to show mercy, do it cheerfully.

ROMANS 12:6–8 TNIV

There is one body and one Spirit — just as you were called to one hope when you were called — one Lord, one faith, one baptism; one God and Father of all, who is over all and through all and in all.

EPHESIANS 4:4–6

God placed all things under [Christ's] feet and appointed him to be head over everything for the church, which is his body, the fullness of him who fills everything in every way.

EPHESIANS 1:22–23

Is anyone among you sick? Let them call the elders of the church to pray over them and anoint them with oil in the name of the Lord. And the prayer offered in faith will make them well.

JAMES 5:14–15 TNIV

Comfort

Praise be to the God and Father of our Lord Jesus Christ, the Father of compassion and the God of all comfort, who comforts us in all our troubles, so that we can comfort those in any trouble with the comfort we ourselves have received from God.

2 CORINTHIANS 1:3–4

The LORD is close to the brokenhearted
*   and saves those who are crushed in spirit.*

PSALM 34:18

Even though I walk
*   through the valley of the shadow of death,*
I will fear no evil,
*   for you are with me;*
your rod and your staff,
*   they comfort me.*

PSALM 23:4

May your unfailing love be my comfort,
*   according to your promise to your servant.*

PSALM 119:76

Comfort

Comfort, comfort my people,
*   says your God.*
Speak tenderly to Jerusalem,
*   and proclaim to her*
that her hard service has been completed,
*   that her sin has been paid for,*
that she has received from the LORD's hand
*   double for all her sins.*

ISAIAH 40:1–2

[Jesus'] disciples came to him, and he began to
teach them, saying:

"Blessed are those who mourn,
*   for they will be comforted."*

MATTHEW 5:1–2, 4

The LORD will surely comfort Zion
*   and will look with compassion on all her ruins;*
he will make her deserts like Eden,
*   her wastelands like the garden of the LORD.*
Joy and gladness will be found in her,
*   thanksgiving and the sound of singing.*

ISAIAH 51:3

Comfort

You turned my wailing into dancing;
*   you removed my sackcloth and clothed me*
*   with joy,*
that my heart may sing to you and not be silent.
*   O LORD my God, I will give you thanks forever.*

PSALM 30:11–12

The Lamb at the center of the throne will be
*   their shepherd;*
*   he will lead them to springs of living water.*
And God will wipe away every tear from their eyes.

REVELATION 7:17

I remember your ancient laws, O LORD,
*   and I find comfort in them.*

PSALM 119:52

The ransomed of the LORD will return.
*   They will enter Zion with singing;*
*   everlasting joy will crown their heads.*
Gladness and joy will overtake them,
*   and sorrow and sighing will flee away.*

ISAIAH 51:11

Comfort

Give me a sign of your goodness,
  that my enemies may see it and be put to shame,
  for you, O LORD, have helped me and
    comforted me.

PSALM 86:17

As a mother comforts her child,
  so will I comfort you;
  and you will be comforted over Jerusalem.

ISAIAH 66:13

Shout for joy, O heavens;
  rejoice, O earth;
  burst into song, O mountains!
For the LORD comforts his people
  and will have compassion on his afflicted ones.

ISAIAH 49:13

"Let the beloved of the LORD rest secure in him,
  for he shields him all day long,
  and the one the LORD loves rests between
    his shoulders."

DEUTERONOMY 33:12

Comfort

The Spirit of the Sovereign LORD is on me,
*   because the LORD has anointed me*
*   to preach good news to the poor.*
He has sent me to bind up the brokenhearted,
*   to proclaim freedom for the captives*
*   and release from darkness for the prisoners...*
to comfort all who mourn,
*   and provide for those who grieve in Zion—*
to bestow on them a crown of beauty
*   instead of ashes,*
the oil of gladness
*   instead of mourning,*
and a garment of praise
*   instead of a spirit of despair.*

ISAIAH 61:1–3

When anxiety was great within me,
*   your consolation brought joy to my soul.*

PSALM 94:19

Comfort

My comfort in my suffering is this:
Your promise preserves my life.

PSALM 119:50

Maidens will dance and be glad,
young men and old as well.
I will turn their mourning into gladness;
I will give them comfort and joy instead
of sorrow.

JEREMIAH 31:13

"I have seen their ways, but I will heal them;
I will guide them and restore comfort to them,
creating praise on the lips of the mourners
in Israel.
Peace, peace, to those far and near,"
says the LORD. "And I will heal them."

ISAIAH 57:18–19 TNIV

You will increase my honor
and comfort me once again.
I will praise you with the harp
for your faithfulness, O my God.

PSALM 71:21–22

Confidence

Jesus said, "I give [my sheep] eternal life, and they shall never perish; no one can snatch them out of my hand. My Father, who has given them to me, is greater than all; no one can snatch them out of my Father's hand."

JOHN 10:28–29

"Though the mountains be shaken
and the hills be removed,
yet my unfailing love for you will not be shaken
nor my covenant of peace be removed,"
says the LORD, who has compassion on you.

ISAIAH 54:10

Since we have confidence to enter the Most Holy Place by the blood of Jesus, let us draw near to God with a sincere heart in full assurance of faith, having our hearts sprinkled to cleanse us from a guilty conscience and having our bodies washed with pure water.

HEBREWS 10:19, 22

Faith is being sure of what we hope for and certain of what we do not see.

HEBREWS 11:1

Confidence

I am not ashamed, because I know whom I have
believed, and am convinced that he is able to guard
what I have entrusted to him for that day.

2 TIMOTHY 1:12

I am convinced that neither death nor life, neither
angels nor demons, neither the present nor the
future, nor any powers, neither height nor depth, nor
anything else in all creation, will be able to separate us from the love of God that is in Christ Jesus
our Lord.

ROMANS 8:38–39

We want each of you to show this same diligence to
the very end, in order to make your hope sure. We
do not want you to become lazy, but to imitate those
who through faith and patience inherit what has
been promised.

HEBREWS 6:11–12

We know and rely on the love God has for us. God is
love. Whoever lives in love lives in God, and God in
him. In this way, love is made complete among us so
that we will have confidence on the day of judgment,
because in this world we are like him.

1 JOHN 4:16–17

Confidence

Jesus declared, "All that the Father gives me will come to me, and whoever comes to me I will never drive away. For I have come down from heaven not to do my will but to do the will of him who sent me. And this is the will of him who sent me, that I shall lose none of all that he has given me, but raise them up at the last day."

JOHN 6:37–39

[Be] confident of this, that he who began a good work in you will carry it on to completion until the day of Christ Jesus.

PHILIPPIANS 1:6

The effect of righteousness will be quietness and confidence forever.

ISAIAH 32:17

Those who have served well gain an excellent standing and great assurance in their faith in Christ Jesus.

1 TIMOTHY 3:13

Confidence

The LORD will be your confidence
and will keep your foot from being snared.

PROVERBS 3:26

This is the confidence we have in approaching God: that if we ask anything according to his will, he hears us. And if we know that he hears us — whatever we ask — we know that we have what we asked of him.

1 JOHN 5:14–15

Let us then approach the throne of grace with confidence, so that we may receive mercy and find grace to help us in our time of need.

HEBREWS 4:16

I am still confident of this:
I will see the goodness of the LORD
in the land of the living.

PSALM 27:13

Confidence

You have been my hope, O Sovereign LORD,
   my confidence since my youth.

PSALM 71:5

This is what the LORD says: ...

"Blessed are those who trust in the LORD,
   whose confidence is in him."

JEREMIAH 17:5, 7 TNIV

The Lord is the stronghold of my life —
   of whom shall I be afraid?
Though an army besiege me,
   my heart will not fear;
though war break out against me,
   even then will I be confident.

PSALM 27:1, 3

Such confidence as this is ours through Christ
before God. Not that we are competent in ourselves
to claim anything for ourselves, but our competence
comes from God.

2 CORINTHIANS 3:4–5

Confidence

I can do everything through [Christ] who gives
me strength.

PHILIPPIANS 4:13

We have come to share in Christ if we hold firmly
till the end the confidence we had at first.

HEBREWS 3:14

If our hearts do not condemn us, we have confidence before God and receive from him anything we
ask, because we obey his commands and do what
pleases him. And this is his command: to believe in
the name of his Son, Jesus Christ, and to love one
another as he commanded us.

1 JOHN 3:21–23

We say with confidence,
   "The Lord is my helper; I will not be afraid.
   What can human beings do to me?"

HEBREWS 13:6 TNIV

God ... has given us the Spirit as a deposit, guaranteeing what is to come. Therefore we are always
confident and know that as long as we are at home
in the body we are away from the Lord.

2 CORINTHIANS 5:5–6

Contentment

Godliness with contentment is great gain. For we brought nothing into the world, and we can take nothing out of it. But if we have food and clothing, we will be content with that.

1 TIMOTHY 6:6–8

The cheerful heart has a continual feast.

PROVERBS 15:15

From the fruit of their mouths people's stomachs
*   are filled;*
*   with the harvest of their lips they are satisfied.*

PROVERBS 18:20 TNIV

Better a little with the fear of the LORD
*   than great wealth with turmoil.*

PROVERBS 15:16

The sluggard craves and gets nothing,
*   but the desires of the diligent are fully satisfied.*

PROVERBS 13:4

Contentment

Better the little that the righteous have
than the wealth of many wicked;
for the power of the wicked will be broken,
but the LORD upholds the righteous.

PSALM 37:16–17

This is what I have observed to be good: that it is
appropriate for people to eat, to drink and to find
satisfaction in their toilsome labor under the sun
during the few days of life God has given them — for
this is their lot.

ECCLESIASTES 5:18 TNIV

A happy heart makes the face cheerful.

PROVERBS 15:13

Better a little with righteousness
than much gain with injustice.

PROVERBS 16:8

I in righteousness I will see your face;
when I awake, I will be satisfied with seeing
your likeness.

PSALM 17:15

Contentment

I am not saying this because I am in need, for I have
learned to be content whatever the circumstances.
I know what it is to be in need, and I know what it
is to have plenty. I have learned the secret of being
content in any and every situation, whether well fed
or hungry, whether living in plenty or in want.

PHILIPPIANS 4:11–12

The fear of the LORD leads to life:
    Then one rests content, untouched by trouble.

PROVERBS 19:23

Keep your lives free from the love of money and be
content with what you have, because God has said,

"Never will I leave you;
    never will I forsake you."

HEBREWS 13:5

Better a dry crust with peace and quiet
    than a house full of feasting, with strife.

PROVERBS 17:1

Contentment

He fulfills the desires of those who fear him;
he hears their cry and saves them.

PSALM 145:19

Better one handful with tranquillity
than two handfuls with toil
and chasing after the wind.

ECCLESIASTES 4:6

LORD, you have assigned me my portion and my cup;
you have made my lot secure.
The boundary lines have fallen for me in
pleasant places;
surely I have a delightful inheritance.

PSALM 16:5–6

The eyes of all look to you,
and you give them their food at the proper time.
You open your hand
and satisfy the desires of every living thing.

PSALM 145:15–16

Contentment

Be still before the LORD
*   and wait patiently for him;*
do not fret when people succeed in their ways,
*   when they carry out their wicked schemes.*
Refrain from anger and turn from wrath;
*   do not fret—it leads only to evil.*
For those who are evil will be destroyed,
*   but those who hope in the LORD will inherit*
*   the land.*

PSALM 37:7–9 TNIV

Jesus said, "Do not store up for yourselves treasures on earth, where moth and rust destroy, and where thieves break in and steal. But store up for yourselves treasures in heaven, where moth and rust do not destroy, and where thieves do not break in and steal. For where your treasure is, there your heart will be also."

MATTHEW 6:19–21

So I commend the enjoyment of life, because there is nothing better for people under the sun than to eat and drink and be glad. Then joy will accompany them in their toil all the days of the life God has given them under the sun.

ECCLESIASTES 8:15 TNIV

Contentment

My soul will be satisfied as with the richest of foods;
with singing lips my mouth will praise you.

PSALM 63:5

The LORD says,
"If my people would but listen to me...
you would be fed with the finest of wheat;
with honey from the rock I would satisfy you."

PSALM 81:13, 16

"Because they love me," says the LORD ...
"With long life will I satisfy them
and show them my salvation."

PSALM 91:14, 16 TNIV

[The LORD] satisfies your desires with good things
so that your youth is renewed like the eagle's.

PSALM 103:5

[The LORD] satisfies the thirsty
and fills the hungry with good things.

PSALM 107:9

Daily Walk

To the Jews who had believed him, Jesus said, "If you hold to my teaching, you are really my disciples. Then you will know the truth, and the truth will set you free."

JOHN 8:31–32

Jesus said, "If anyone gives even a cup of cold water to one of these little ones who is known to be my disciple, truly I tell you, that person will certainly be rewarded."

MATTHEW 10:42 TNIV

Jesus said to his disciples, "Whoever wants to be my disciple must deny themselves and take up their cross and follow me. For whoever wants to save their life will lose it, but whoever loses their life for me will find it."

MATTHEW 16:24–25 TNIV

Jesus said, "A new command I give you: Love one another. As I have loved you, so you must love one another. By this everyone will know that you are my disciples, if you love one another."

JOHN 13:34–35 TNIV

Daily Walk

We pray this in order that you may live a life worthy of the Lord and may please him in every way: bearing fruit in every good work, growing in the knowledge of God.

COLOSSIANS 1:10

Be very careful, then, how you live — not as unwise but as wise.

EPHESIANS 5:15

Those who walk righteously
    and speak what is right,
who reject gain from extortion
    and keep their hands from accepting bribes,
who stop their ears against plots of murder
    and shut their eyes against contemplating evil —
they are the ones who will dwell on the heights,
    whose refuge will be the mountain fortress.
Their bread will be supplied,
    and water will not fail them.

ISAIAH 33:15 – 16 TNIV

Daily Walk

Jesus said, "Whoever serves me must follow me; and where I am, my servant also will be. My Father will honor the one who serves me."

JOHN 12:26

Jesus said, "I am the light of the world. Whoever follows me will never walk in darkness, but will have the light of life."

JOHN 8:12

Jesus said, "This is to my Father's glory, that you bear much fruit, showing yourselves to be my disciples."

JOHN 15:8

I urge you, brothers and sisters, in view of God's mercy, to offer your bodies as a living sacrifice, holy and pleasing to God—this is true worship. Do not conform to the pattern of this world, but be transformed by the renewing of your mind. Then you will be able to test and approve what God's will is—his good, pleasing and perfect will.

ROMANS 12:1–2 TNIV

Daily Walk

The one who sows to please the Spirit, from the Spirit will reap eternal life.

GALATIANS 6:8

"You who revere my name, the sun of righteousness will rise with healing in its wings," says the LORD.

MALACHI 4:2

Do your best to present yourself to God as one approved,... and who correctly handles the word of truth.

2 TIMOTHY 2:15

Christ suffered for you, leaving you an example, that you should follow in his steps.

1 PETER 2:21

We are the temple of the living God. As God has said: "I will live with them and walk among them, and I will be their God, and they will be my people."

"Therefore come out from them
and be separate, says the Lord.
Touch no unclean thing,
and I will receive you."

2 CORINTHIANS 6:16–17

Daily Walk

Since we live by the Spirit, let us keep in step with the Spirit.

GALATIANS 5:25

God did not call us to be impure, but to live a holy life.

1 THESSALONIANS 4:7

This is what the LORD says:

"Stand at the crossroads and look;
*   ask for the ancient paths,*
ask where the good way is, and walk in it,
*   and you will find rest for your souls."*

JEREMIAH 6:16

Walk in all the way that the LORD your God has commanded you, so that you may live and prosper and prolong your days in the land that you will possess.

DEUTERONOMY 5:33

Whoever claims to live in him must walk as Jesus did.

1 JOHN 2:6

Daily Walk

Jesus said, "Remain in me, as I also remain in you. No branch can bear fruit by itself; it must remain in the vine. Neither can you bear fruit unless you remain in me. I am the vine; you are the branches. If you remain in me and I in you, you will bear much fruit; apart from me you can do nothing."

JOHN 15:4–5 TNIV

If they obey and serve him,
> *they will spend the rest of their days in prosperity*
> *and their years in contentment.*

JOB 36:11

Jesus said, "You did not choose me, but I chose you and appointed you to go and bear fruit — fruit that will last."

JOHN 15:16

He holds victory in store for the upright,
> *he is a shield to those whose walk is blameless,*
for he guards the course of the just
> *and protects the way of his faithful ones.*

PROVERBS 2:7–8

Emotions

A bruised reed he will not break,
*   and a smoldering wick he will not snuff out.*
In faithfulness he will bring forth justice.

ISAIAH 42:3

He was despised and rejected by others,
*   a man of suffering, and familiar with pain.*
Like one from whom people hide their faces
*   he was despised, and we held him in low esteem.*
Surely he took up our pain
*   and bore our suffering.*

ISAIAH 53:3–4 TNIV

The cords of death entangled me,
*   the anguish of the grave came upon me;*
*   I was overcome by trouble and sorrow.*
Then I called on the name of the LORD:
*   "O LORD, save me!"*
The LORD is gracious and righteous;
*   our God is full of compassion.*
The LORD protects the simplehearted;
*   when I was in great need, he saved me.*

PSALM 116:3–6

Emotions

Who shall separate us from the love of Christ? Shall
trouble or hardship or persecution or famine or nakedness or danger or sword? No, in all these things
we are more than conquerors through him who
loved us.

ROMANS 8:35, 37

We do not want you to be uninformed about those
who sleep in death, so that you do not grieve like
the rest, who have no hope. We believe that Jesus
died and rose again, and so we believe that God will
bring with Jesus those who have fallen asleep
in him.

1 THESSALONIANS 4:13 – 14 TNIV

I heard a loud voice from the throne saying, "Look!
God's dwelling place is now among the people, and
he will dwell with them. They will be his people,
and God himself will be with them and be their
God. 'He will wipe every tear from their eyes. There
will be no more death' or mourning or crying or
pain, for the old order of things has passed away."

REVELATION 21:3 – 4 TNIV

I will refresh the weary and satisfy the faint.

JEREMIAH 31:25

Emotions

Why are you downcast, O my soul?
Why so disturbed within me?
Put your hope in God,
for I will yet praise him,
my Savior and my God.

PSALM 42:5–6

You, O LORD, have delivered my soul from death,
my eyes from tears,
my feet from stumbling.

PSALM 116:8

My soul is downcast within me.
Yet this I call to mind
and therefore I have hope:
Because of the LORD's great love we are
not consumed,
for his compassions never fail.
They are new every morning;
great is your faithfulness.

LAMENTATIONS 3:20–23

Emotions

He will swallow up death forever.
The Sovereign LORD will wipe away the tears
    from all faces;
he will remove the disgrace of his people
    from all the earth.

ISAIAH 25:8

"Restrain your voice from weeping
    and your eyes from tears,
for your work will be rewarded,"
        declares the LORD.

JEREMIAH 31:16

Even though I walk
    through the valley of the shadow of death,
I will fear no evil,
    for you are with me;
your rod and your staff,
    they comfort me.

PSALM 23:4

Emotions

Those who sow in tears
will reap with songs of joy.

PSALM 126:5

My flesh and my heart may fail,
but God is the strength of my heart
and my portion forever.

PSALM 73:26

Jesus said,
"*Blessed are those who mourn,*
for they will be comforted."

MATTHEW 5:4

Do not fear, for I am with you;
do not be dismayed, for I am your God.
I will strengthen you and help you;
I will uphold you with my righteous right hand.

ISAIAH 41:10

Emotions

My eyes grow weak with sorrow;
    they fail because of all my foes.
Away from me, all you who do evil,
    for the LORD has heard my weeping.
The LORD has heard my cry for mercy;
    the LORD accepts my prayer.

PSALM 6:7–9

The ransomed of the LORD will return.
They will enter Zion with singing;
    everlasting joy will crown their heads.
Gladness and joy will overtake them,
    and sorrow and sighing will flee away.

ISAIAH 35:10

I will turn their mourning into gladness;
    I will give them comfort and joy instead
        of sorrow.

JEREMIAH 31:13

Eternal Life

Jesus declared, "God so loved the world that he gave his one and only Son, that whoever believes in him shall not perish but have eternal life."

JOHN 3:16

The world and its desires pass away, but whoever does the will of God lives forever.

1 JOHN 2:17 TNIV

The gift of God is eternal life in Christ Jesus our Lord.

ROMANS 6:23

"Whoever believes in the Son has eternal life."

JOHN 3:36

Jesus said, "This is eternal life: that they may know you, the only true God, and Jesus Christ, whom you have sent."

JOHN 17:3

Once made perfect, [Jesus] became the source of eternal salvation for all who obey him.

HEBREWS 5:9

Eternal Life

God has given us eternal life, and this life is in his Son. Whoever has the Son has life.

1 JOHN 5:11–12 TNIV

Jesus said, "I give [my sheep] eternal life, and they shall never perish; no one can snatch them out of my hand."

JOHN 10:28

Jesus said, "I am the resurrection and the life. Anyone who believes in me will live, even though they die; and whoever lives by believing in me will never die."

JOHN 11:25–26 TNIV

Jesus said, "Everyone who has left houses or brothers or sisters or father or mother or children or fields for my sake will receive a hundred times as much and will inherit eternal life."

MATTHEW 19:29

Jesus said, "Just as Moses lifted up the snake in the desert, so the Son of Man must be lifted up, that everyone who believes in him may have eternal life."

JOHN 3:14–15

Eternal Life

Jesus said, "Whoever believes has eternal life."

JOHN 6:47 TNIV

Jesus answered, "Everyone who drinks this water will be thirsty again, but those who drink the water I give them will never thirst. Indeed, the water I give them will become in them a spring of water welling up to eternal life."

JOHN 4:13–14 TNIV

Christ was sacrificed once to take away the sins of many people; and he will appear a second time, not to bear sin, but to bring salvation to those who are waiting for him.

HEBREWS 9:28

Jesus said, "In my Father's house are many rooms.... I am going there to prepare a place for you. And if I go and prepare a place for you, I will come back and take you to be with me that you also may be where I am."

JOHN 14:2–3

We know that if the earthly tent we live in is destroyed, we have a building from God, an eternal house in heaven, not built by human hands.

2 CORINTHIANS 5:1

Eternal Life

Jesus said, "Rejoice that your names are written in heaven."

LUKE 10:20

I saw "a new heaven and a new earth," for the first heaven and the first earth had passed away, and there was no longer any sea.... I heard a loud voice from the throne saying, "Look! God's dwelling place is now among the people, and he will dwell with them. They will be his people, and God himself will be with them and be their God. 'He will wipe every tear from their eyes. There will be no more death' or mourning or crying or pain, for the old order of things has passed away."

REVELATION 21:1, 3–4 TNIV

"Never again will they hunger;
    never again will they thirst.
The sun will not beat upon them,
    nor any scorching heat.
For the Lamb at the center of the throne will be their shepherd;
    he will lead them to springs of living water.
And God will wipe away every tear from their eyes."

REVELATION 7:16–17

Eternal Life

Keep yourselves in God's love as you wait for the mercy of our Lord Jesus Christ to bring you to eternal life.

JUDE 21

The Lord himself will come down from heaven, with a loud command, with the voice of the archangel and with the trumpet call of God, and the dead in Christ will rise first. After that, we who are still alive and are left will be caught up together with them in the clouds to meet the Lord in the air. And so we will be with the Lord forever.

1 THESSALONIANS 4:16–17

Jesus said, "The sign of the Son of Man will appear in the sky, and all the nations of the earth will mourn. They will see the Son of Man coming on the clouds of the sky, with power and great glory. And he will send his angels with a loud trumpet call, and they will gather his elect from the four winds, from one end of the heavens to the other."

MATTHEW 24:30–31

Eternal Life

The day of the Lord will come like a thief. The heavens will disappear with a roar; the elements will be destroyed by fire, and the earth and everything in it will be laid bare.

2 PETER 3:10

Jesus said, "This gospel of the kingdom will be preached in the whole world as a testimony to all nations, and then the end will come."

MATTHEW 24:14

The throne of God and of the Lamb will be in the city, and his servants will serve him. They will see his face, and his name will be on their foreheads. There will be no more night. They will not need the light of a lamp or the light of the sun, for the Lord God will give them light. And they will reign for ever and ever.

REVELATION 22:3–5

Our citizenship is in heaven. And we eagerly await a Savior from there, the Lord Jesus Christ, who, by the power that enables him to bring everything under his control, will transform our lowly bodies so that they will be like his glorious body.

PHILIPPIANS 3:20–21

Evangelism

Jesus said to them, "Go into all the world and preach the good news to all creation."

MARK 16:15

It is written: "I believed; therefore I have spoken." With that same spirit of faith we also believe and therefore speak.

2 CORINTHIANS 4:13

We proclaim him, admonishing and teaching everyone with all wisdom, so that we may present everyone perfect in Christ.

COLOSSIANS 1:28

I pray that you may be active in sharing your faith, so that you will have a full understanding of every good thing we have in Christ.

PHILEMON 1:6

In your hearts set apart Christ as Lord. Always be prepared to give an answer to everyone who asks you to give the reason for the hope that you have. But do this with gentleness and respect.

1 PETER 3:15

Evangelism

Jesus said, "No one lights a lamp and hides it in a clay jar or puts it under a bed. Instead, they put it on a stand, so that those who come in can see the light."

LUKE 8:16 TNIV

Jesus said, "Whoever publicly acknowledges me I will also acknowledge before my Father in heaven."

MATTHEW 10:32 TNIV

How beautiful on the mountains
*   are the feet of those who bring good news,*
who proclaim peace,
*   who bring good tidings,*
*   who proclaim salvation,*
who say to Zion,
*   "Your God reigns!"*

ISAIAH 52:7

They were all filled with the Holy Spirit and spoke the word of God boldly.

ACTS 4:31

Evangelism

My mouth will tell of your righteousness,
*   of your salvation all day long,...*
I will come and proclaim your mighty acts,
*   O Sovereign LORD;*
*   I will proclaim your righteousness, yours alone.*

PSALM 71:15–16

Peter and John said, "Now, Lord ... enable your
servants to speak your word with great boldness.
Stretch out your hand to heal and perform miraculous signs and wonders through the name of your
holy servant Jesus."

ACTS 4:29–30

Even when I am old and gray,
*   do not forsake me, O God,*
till I declare your power to the next generation,
*   your might to all who are to come.*

PSALM 71:18

I am not ashamed of the gospel, because it is the
power of God for the salvation of everyone
who believes.

ROMANS 1:16

Evangelism

Give thanks to the LORD, call on his name;
make known among the nations what he
has done.
Sing to him, sing praise to him;
tell of all his wonderful acts.

PSALM 105:1–2

Jesus said, "All authority in heaven and on earth has been given to me. Therefore go and make disciples of all nations, baptizing them in the name of the Father and of the Son and of the Holy Spirit, and teaching them to obey everything I have commanded you. And surely I am with you always, to the very end of the age."

MATTHEW 28:18–20

Jesus said, "This gospel of the kingdom will be preached in the whole world as a testimony to all nations, and then the end will come."

MATTHEW 24:14

Boldly and without hindrance [Paul] preached the kingdom of God and taught about the Lord Jesus Christ.

ACTS 28:31

Evangelism

Jesus said, "You are the light of the world. A city on a hill cannot be hidden. Neither do people light a lamp and put it under a bowl. Instead they put it on its stand, and it gives light to everyone in the house. In the same way, let your light shine before others, that they may see your good deeds and glorify your Father in heaven."

MATTHEW 5:14–16 TNIV

I pray that you may be active in sharing your faith, so that you will have a full understanding of every good thing we have in Christ.

PHILEMON 1:6

Paul said: "I consider my life worth nothing to me, if only I may finish the race and complete the task the Lord Jesus has given me—the task of testifying to the gospel of God's grace."

ACTS 20:24

Jesus said, "You will receive power when the Holy Spirit comes on you; and you will be my witnesses in Jerusalem, and in all Judea and Samaria, and to the ends of the earth."

ACTS 1:8

Evangelism

We are therefore Christ's ambassadors, as though God were making his appeal through us. We implore you on Christ's behalf: Be reconciled to God.

2 CORINTHIANS 5:20

Pray also for me, that whenever I open my mouth, words may be given me so that I will fearlessly make known the mystery of the gospel, for which I am an ambassador in chains. Pray that I may declare it fearlessly, as I should.

EPHESIANS 6:19–20

All this is from God, who reconciled us to himself through Christ and gave us the ministry of reconciliation: that God was reconciling the world to himself in Christ, not counting people's sins against them. And he has committed to us the message of reconciliation.

2 CORINTHIANS 5:18–19 TNIV

I will praise you, O LORD, with all my heart;
I will tell of all your wonders.

PSALM 9:1

Faith and Trust

Jesus replied, "I tell you the truth, if you have faith and do not doubt, not only can you do what was done to the fig tree, but also you can say to this mountain, 'Go, throw yourself into the sea,' and it will be done."

MATTHEW 21:21

Jesus said, "I tell you, whatever you ask for in prayer, believe that you have received it, and it will be yours."

MARK 11:24

Jesus said, "According to your faith will it be done to you."

MATTHEW 9:29

Jesus said, "Satan has asked to sift you as wheat. But I have prayed for you, Simon, that your faith may not fail."

LUKE 22:31–32

Jesus said, "Very truly I tell you, all who have faith in me will do the works I have been doing, and they will do even greater things than these, because I am going to the Father."

JOHN 14:12 TNIV

Faith and Trust

Some trust in chariots and some in horses,
but we trust in the name of the LORD our God.

PSALM 20:7

My salvation and my honor depend on God;
he is my mighty rock, my refuge.

PSALM 62:7

May your unfailing love rest upon us, O LORD,
even as we put our hope in you.

PSALM 33:22

The law of the LORD is perfect,
reviving the soul.
The statutes of the LORD are trustworthy,
making wise the simple.

PSALM 19:7

Faith is being sure of what we hope for and certain
of what we do not see.

HEBREWS 11:1

Faith and Trust

What does the Scripture say? "Abraham believed God, and it was credited to him as righteousness."

ROMANS 4:3

Since we have been justified through faith, we have peace with God through our Lord Jesus Christ.

ROMANS 5:1

Through [Christ] you believe in God, who raised him from the dead and glorified him, and so your faith and hope are in God.

1 PETER 1:21

Though you have not seen [Christ], you love him; and even though you do not see him now, you believe in him and are filled with an inexpressible and glorious joy.

1 PETER 1:8

This is a trustworthy saying that deserves full acceptance. That is why we labor and strive, because we have put our hope in the living God, who is the Savior of all people, and especially of those who believe.

1 TIMOTHY 4:9–10 TNIV

Faith and Trust

Trust in the LORD with all your heart
*   and lean not on your own understanding;*
in all your ways acknowledge him,
*   and he will make your paths straight.*

PROVERBS 3:5–6

I do not trust in my bow,
*   my sword does not bring me victory;*
but you give us victory over our enemies,
*   you put our adversaries to shame.*

PSALM 44:6–7

Build yourselves up in your most holy faith and pray
in the Holy Spirit. Keep yourselves in God's love as
you wait for the mercy of our Lord Jesus Christ to
bring you to eternal life.

JUDE 1:20–21

Those who know your name will trust in you,
*   for you, LORD, have never forsaken those who*
*   seek you.*

PSALM 9:10

Faith and Trust

I trust in your unfailing love;
my heart rejoices in your salvation.

PSALM 13:5

In you our fathers put their trust;
they trusted and you delivered them.
They cried to you and were saved;
in you they trusted and were not disappointed.

PSALM 22:4–5

The LORD is my strength and my shield;
my heart trusts in him, and I am helped.

PSALM 28:7

You brought me out of the womb;
you made me trust in you
even at my mother's breast.

PSALM 22:9

Faith and Trust

It is by grace you have been saved, through faith—and this not from yourselves, it is the gift of God—not by works, so that no one can boast.

EPHESIANS 2:8–9

Faith comes from hearing the message, and the message is heard through the word of Christ.

ROMANS 10:17

Take up the shield of faith, with which you can extinguish all the flaming arrows of the evil one.

EPHESIANS 6:16

[Abraham] did not waver through unbelief regarding the promise of God, but was strengthened in his faith and gave glory to God, being fully persuaded that God had power to do what he had promised.

ROMANS 4:20–21

We live by faith, not by sight.

2 CORINTHIANS 5:7

Faithfulness

Jesus said, "His master replied, 'Well done, good and faithful servant! You have been faithful with a few things; I will put you in charge of many things. Come and share your master's happiness!'"

MATTHEW 25:21

Be joyful in hope, patient in affliction, faithful in prayer.

ROMANS 12:12

It is required that those who have been given a trust must prove faithful.

1 CORINTHIANS 4:2

The fruit of the Spirit is ... faithfulness.

GALATIANS 5:22

I thank Christ Jesus our Lord, who has given me strength, that he considered me faithful, appointing me to his service.

1 TIMOTHY 1:12

To the faithful you show yourself faithful.

PSALM 18:25

Faithfulness

Each of you should use whatever gift you have received to serve others, as faithful stewards of God's grace in its various forms.

1 PETER 4:10 TNIV

They will make war against the Lamb, but the Lamb will overcome them because he is Lord of lords and King of kings—and with him will be his called, chosen and faithful followers.

REVELATION 17:14

Love the LORD, all his saints!
  The LORD preserves the faithful,
  but the proud he pays back in full.

PSALM 31:23

The LORD loves the just
  and will not forsake his faithful ones.
They will be protected forever,
  but the offspring of the wicked will be cut off.

PSALM 37:28

Faithfulness

Let those who love the LORD hate evil,
   for he guards the lives of his faithful ones
   and delivers them from the hand of the wicked.

PSALM 97:10

My eyes will be on the faithful in the land,
   that they may dwell with me;
those whose walk is blameless
   will minister to me.

PSALM 101:6 TNIV

The faithless will be fully repaid for their ways,
   and the good rewarded for theirs.

PROVERBS 14:14 TNIV

Many claim to have unfailing love,
   but a faithful person who can find?

PROVERBS 20:6 TNIV

Faithfulness

Let love and faithfulness never leave you;
bind them around your neck,
write them on the tablet of your heart.
Then you will win favor and a good name
in the sight of God and humankind.

PROVERBS 3:3–4 TNIV

Love and faithfulness keep a king safe;
through love his throne is made secure.

PROVERBS 20:28

A faithful person will be richly blessed,
but one eager to get rich will not go unpunished.

PROVERBS 28:20 TNIV

Lazy hands make for poverty,
but diligent hands bring wealth.

PROVERBS 10:4 TNIV

Faithfulness

Diligent hands will rule,
but laziness ends in slave labor.

PROVERBS 12:24

The sluggard craves and gets nothing,
but the desires of the diligent are fully satisfied.

PROVERBS 13:4

The plans of the diligent lead to profit
as surely as haste leads to poverty.

PROVERBS 21:5

Don't let anyone look down on you because you
are young, but set an example for the believers in
speech, in life, in love, in faith and in purity....
Devote yourself to the public reading of Scripture,
to preaching and to teaching. Do not neglect your
gift.... Be diligent in these matters; give yourself
wholly to them, so that everyone may see your prog-
ress. Watch your life and doctrine closely. Persevere in them, because if you do, you will save both
yourself and your hearers.

1 TIMOTHY 4:12–16

Faithfulness

Those who work their land will have abundant food,
but those who chase fantasies have no sense.

PROVERBS 12:11 TNIV

All hard work brings a profit,
but mere talk leads only to poverty.

PROVERBS 14:23

The appetite of laborers works for them;
their hunger drives them on.

PROVERBS 16:26 TNIV

A wife of noble character ...
works with eager hands.
She sets about her work vigorously;
her arms are strong for her tasks.
She sees that her trading is profitable,
and her lamp does not go out at night.
Give her the reward she has earned,
and let her works bring her praise at the
city gate.

PROVERBS 31:10, 13, 17–18, 31

Forgiveness

Blessed are those
whose transgressions are forgiven,
whose sins are covered.
Blessed are those
whose sin the LORD does not count against them
and in whose spirit is no deceit.

PSALM 32:1–2 TNIV

Praise the LORD, O my soul,
and forget not all his benefits—
who forgives all your sins.

PSALM 103:2–3

If you, O LORD, kept a record of sins,
O Lord, who could stand?
But with you there is forgiveness;
therefore you are feared.

PSALM 130:3–4

Forgiveness

Who is a God like you,
who pardons sin and forgives the transgression
of the remnant of his inheritance?
You do not stay angry forever
but delight to show mercy.

MICAH 7:18

Jesus said, "If you forgive others when they sin against you, your heavenly Father will also forgive you. But if you do not forgive others their sins, your Father will not forgive your sins."

MATTHEW 6:14–15 TNIV

Peter came to Jesus and asked, "Lord, how many times shall I forgive someone who sins against me? Up to seven times?" Jesus answered, "I tell you, not seven times, but seventy-seven times."

MATTHEW 18:21–22 TNIV

Jesus said, "This is my blood of the covenant, which is poured out for many for the forgiveness of sins."

MATTHEW 26:28

Forgiveness

Jesus said, "Do not judge, and you will not be judged. Do not condemn, and you will not be condemned. Forgive, and you will be forgiven."

LUKE 6:37

Jesus said, "If a brother or sister sins against you, rebuke them; and if they repent, forgive them. Even if they sin against you seven times in a day and seven times come back to you saying 'I repent,' you must forgive them."

LUKE 17:3–4 TNIV

I want you to know that through Jesus the forgiveness of sins is proclaimed to you. Through him everyone who believes is justified from everything you could not be justified from by the law of Moses.

ACTS 13:38–39

The LORD says,
*"I, even I, am he who blots out
    your transgressions, for my own sake,
    and remembers your sins no more."*

ISAIAH 43:25

Forgiveness

In him we have redemption through his blood, the forgiveness of sins, in accordance with the riches of God's grace.

EPHESIANS 1:7

He has rescued us from the dominion of darkness and brought us into the kingdom of the Son he loves, in whom we have redemption, the forgiveness of sins.

COLOSSIANS 1:13–14

Bear with each other and forgive whatever grievances you may have against one another. Forgive as the Lord forgave you.

COLOSSIANS 3:13

Without the shedding of blood there is no forgiveness.

HEBREWS 9:22

If we confess our sins, he is faithful and just and will forgive us our sins and purify us from all unrighteousness.

1 JOHN 1:9

Forgiveness

I acknowledged my sin to you
and did not cover up my iniquity.
I said, "I will confess
my transgressions to the LORD"—
and you forgave
the guilt of my sin.

PSALM 32:5

Have mercy on me, O God,
according to your unfailing love;
according to your great compassion
blot out my transgressions.
Wash away all my iniquity
and cleanse me from my sin.
For I know my transgressions,
and my sin is always before me.
Against you, you only, have I sinned....
Cleanse me with hyssop, and I will be clean;
wash me, and I will be whiter than snow.

PSALM 51:1–4, 7

Forgiveness

As far as the east is from the west,
    so far has he removed our transgressions from us.

PSALM 103:12

He was pierced for our transgressions,
    he was crushed for our iniquities;
the punishment that brought us peace was upon him,
    and by his wounds we are healed.
We all, like sheep, have gone astray,
    each of us has turned to his own way;
and the LORD has laid on him
    the iniquity of us all.

ISAIAH 53:5–6

"Blessed are those
    whose transgressions are forgiven,
    whose sins are covered.
Blessed are those
    whose sin the Lord will never count
        against them."

ROMANS 4:7–8 TNIV

Friendship

I am a friend to all who fear you,
to all who follow your precepts.

PSALM 119:63

The righteous choose their friends carefully,
but the way of the wicked leads them astray.

PROVERBS 12:26 TNIV

A friend loves at all times,
and a brother is born for adversity.

PROVERBS 17:17

One who has unreliable friends soon comes to ruin,
but there is a friend who sticks closer than
a brother.

PROVERBS 18:24 TNIV

One who loves a pure heart and who speaks
with grace
will have the king for a friend.

PROVERBS 22:11 TNIV

Friendship

Wounds from a friend can be trusted,
*   but an enemy multiplies kisses.*

PROVERBS 27:6

Do not forsake your friend and the friend of
your father.

PROVERBS 27:10

Two are better than one,
*   because they have a good return for their labor:*
If they fall down,
*   they can help each other up.*
But pity those who fall
*   and have no one to help them up!*
Also, if two lie down together, they will keep warm.
*   But how can one keep warm alone?*
Though one may be overpowered,
*   two can defend themselves.*
A cord of three strands is not quickly broken.

ECCLESIASTES 4:9–12 TNIV

Friendship

Jesus said, "Greater love has no one than this: to lay down one's life for one's friends."

JOHN 15:13 TNIV

Perfume and incense bring joy to the heart,
and the pleasantness of a friend springs from
their heartfelt advice.

PROVERBS 27:9 TNIV

Jesus said, "You are my friends if you do what I command."

JOHN 15:14

When Jesus saw their faith, he said, "Friend, your sins are forgiven."

LUKE 5:20

Jonathan said to David, "Go in peace, for we have sworn friendship with each other in the name of the LORD, saying, 'The LORD is witness between you and me, and between your descendants and my descendants forever.'"

1 SAMUEL 20:42

Dear friends, let us love one another, for love comes from God.

1 JOHN 4:7

Friendship

The scripture was fulfilled that says, "Abraham believed God, and it was credited to him as righteousness," and he was called God's friend.

JAMES 2:23

The LORD would speak to Moses face to face, as one speaks to a friend.

EXODUS 33:11 TNIV

Jesus said, "I no longer call you servants, because a servant does not know his master's business. Instead, I have called you friends, for everything that I learned from my Father I have made known to you."

JOHN 15:15

Do not make friends with the hot-tempered,
    do not associate with those who are
        easily angered,
or you may learn their ways
    and get yourself ensnared.

PROVERBS 22:24–25 TNIV

Dear friends, since God so loved us, we also ought to love one another.

1 JOHN 4:11

Friendship

As iron sharpens iron,
*   so one person sharpens another.*

PROVERBS 27:17 TNIV

Walk with the wise and become wise,
*   for a companion of fools suffers harm.*

PROVERBS 13:20 TNIV

Gossips betray a confidence,
*   but the trustworthy keep a secret.*

PROVERBS 11:13 TNIV

A gossip betrays a confidence;
*   so avoid anyone who talks too much.*

PROVERBS 20:19 TNIV

God, who has called you into fellowship with his
Son Jesus Christ our Lord, is faithful.

1 CORINTHIANS 1:9

Friendship

Do not be yoked together with unbelievers. For what do righteousness and wickedness have in common? Or what fellowship can light have with darkness?

2 CORINTHIANS 6:14

We proclaim to you what we have seen and heard, so that you also may have fellowship with us. And our fellowship is with the Father and with his Son, Jesus Christ.

1 JOHN 1:3

If we claim to have fellowship with him yet walk in the darkness, we lie and do not live by the truth. But if we walk in the light, as he is in the light, we have fellowship with one another, and the blood of Jesus, his Son, purifies us from all sin.

1 JOHN 1:6–7

Be devoted to one another in love. Honor one another above yourselves.

ROMANS 12:10 TNIV

Jesus said, "Here I am! I stand at the door and knock. If anyone hears my voice and opens the door, I will come in and eat with them, and they with me."

REVELATION 3:20 TNIV

Generosity

A generous person will prosper;
  whoever refreshes others will be refreshed.

PROVERBS 11:25 TNIV

Those who give to the poor will lack nothing.

PROVERBS 28:27 TNIV

If anyone is poor among your people ... give generously to them and do so without a grudging heart; then because of this the LORD your God will bless you in all your work and in everything you put your hand to.

DEUTERONOMY 15:7, 10 TNIV

Jesus said, "When you give to the needy, do not let your left hand know what your right hand is doing, so that your giving may be in secret. Then your Father, who sees what is done in secret, will reward you."

MATTHEW 6:3–4

Jesus himself said: "It is more blessed to give than to receive."

ACTS 20:35

Generosity

Jesus said, "If you then, though you are evil, know how to give good gifts to your children, how much more will your Father in heaven give the Holy Spirit to those who ask him!"

LUKE 11:13

Jesus said, "Give, and it will be given to you. A good measure, pressed down, shaken together and running over, will be poured into your lap. For with the measure you use, it will be measured to you."

LUKE 6:38

Each of you should give what you have decided in your heart to give, not reluctantly or under compulsion, for God loves a cheerful giver.

2 CORINTHIANS 9:7 TNIV

Jesus said, "Give to everyone who asks you, and if anyone takes what belongs to you, do not demand it back."

LUKE 6:30

You will be made rich in every way so that you can be generous on every occasion.

2 CORINTHIANS 9:11

Generosity

The generous will themselves be blessed,
   for they share their food with the poor.

PROVERBS 22:9 TNIV

Good will come to those who are generous and
      lend freely,
   who conduct their affairs with justice.

PSALM 112:5 TNIV

Remember this: Whoever sows sparingly will also reap sparingly, and whoever sows generously will also reap generously.

2 CORINTHIANS 9:6

"Bring the whole tithe into the storehouse, that there may be food in my house. Test me in this," says the LORD Almighty, "and see if I will not throw open the floodgates of heaven and pour out so much blessing that you will not have room enough for it."

MALACHI 3:10

Jesus said, "As for what is inside you — be generous to the poor, and everything will be clean for you."

LUKE 11:41 TNIV

Generosity

I was young and now I am old,
   yet I have never seen the righteous forsaken
   or their children begging bread.
They are always generous and lend freely;
   their children will be blessed.

PSALM 37:25–26

Honor the LORD with your wealth,
   with the firstfruits of all your crops;
then your barns will be filled to overflowing,
   and your vats will brim over with new wine.

PROVERBS 3:9–10

David said, "Who am I, and who are my people,
that we should be able to give as generously as this?
Everything comes from you, and we have given you
only what comes from your hand."

1 CHRONICLES 29:14

Jesus said, "Freely you have received, freely give."

MATTHEW 10:8

Generosity

The wicked borrow and do not repay,
but the righteous give generously.

PSALM 37:21

Command [those who are rich in this present world]
to do good, to be rich in good deeds, and to be
generous and willing to share. In this way they will
lay up treasure for themselves as a firm foundation
for the coming age, so that they may take hold of the
life that is truly life.

1 TIMOTHY 6:18–19

Jesus said, "If anyone gives even a cup of cold water
to one of these little ones who is known to be my
disciple, truly I tell you, that person will certainly
be rewarded."

MATTHEW 10:42 TNIV

The angel answered [Cornelius], "Your prayers and
gifts to the poor have come up as a memorial offering before God."

ACTS 10:4

Generosity

Jesus answered, "If you want to be perfect, go, sell your possessions and give to the poor, and you will have treasure in heaven. Then come, follow me."

MATTHEW 19:21

Jesus said, "The King will say to those on his right, 'Come, you who are blessed by my Father; take your inheritance, the kingdom prepared for you since the creation of the world. For I was hungry and you gave me something to eat, I was thirsty and you gave me something to drink, I was a stranger and you invited me in, I needed clothes and you clothed me, I was sick and you looked after me, I was in prison and you came to visit me.... Truly I tell you, whatever you did for one of the least of these brothers and sisters of mine, you did for me.'"

MATTHEW 25:34–36, 40 TNIV

[A wife of noble character] opens her arms to
*   the poor*
* and extends her hands to the needy.*

PROVERBS 31:20

God's Goodness

God saw all that he had made, and it was very good.

GENESIS 1:31

The fruit of the light consists in all goodness, righteousness and truth.

EPHESIANS 5:9 TNIV

His divine power has given us everything we need for a godly life through our knowledge of him who called us by his own glory and goodness.

2 PETER 1:3 TNIV

Surely goodness and love will follow me
all the days of my life,
and I will dwell in the house of the LORD
forever.

PSALM 23:6

Remember not the sins of my youth
and my rebellious ways;
according to your love remember me,
for you are good, O LORD.

PSALM 25:7

God's Goodness

I said to the LORD, "You are my Lord;
   apart from you I have no good thing."

PSALM 16:2

I am still confident of this:
   I will see the goodness of the LORD
   in the land of the living.

PSALM 27:13

How great is your goodness,
   which you have stored up for those who fear you,
which you bestow in the sight of all
   on those who take refuge in you.

PSALM 31:19 TNIV

Good and upright is the LORD;
   therefore he instructs sinners in his ways.

PSALM 25:8

God's Goodness

Taste and see that the LORD is good;
blessed are those who take refuge in him.

PSALM 34:8 TNIV

I will praise you forever for what you have done;
in your name I will hope, for your name is good.
I will praise you in the presence of your saints.

PSALM 52:9

Blessed are those you choose
and bring near to live in your courts!
We are filled with the good things of your house,
of your holy temple.

PSALM 65:4

The lions may grow weak and hungry,
but those who seek the LORD lack no good thing.

PSALM 34:10

God's Goodness

The LORD God is a sun and shield;
*   the LORD bestows favor and honor;*
no good thing does he withhold
*   from those whose walk is blameless.*

PSALM 84:11

You are forgiving and good, O Lord,
*   abounding in love to all who call to you.*

PSALM 86:5

The LORD is good and his love endures forever;
*   his faithfulness continues through*
*   all generations.*

PSALM 100:5

Every good and perfect gift is from above, coming
down from the Father of the heavenly lights.

JAMES 1:17

You are good, and what you do is good.

PSALM 119:68

God's Goodness

Rejoice greatly, O Daughter of Zion!
*   Shout, Daughter of Jerusalem!*
See, your king comes to you,
*   righteous and having salvation,*
*   gentle and riding on a donkey,*
*   on a colt, the foal of a donkey.*

ZECHARIAH 9:9

Jesus said, "Come to me, all you who are weary and burdened, and I will give you rest. Take my yoke upon you and learn from me, for I am gentle and humble in heart, and you will find rest for your souls. For my yoke is easy and my burden is light."

MATTHEW 11:28–30

The fruit of the Spirit is ... goodness ... gentleness.

GALATIANS 5:22–23

Praise the LORD, for the LORD is good;
*   sing praise to his name, for that is pleasant.*

PSALM 135:3

God's Goodness

Teach me to do your will,
*   for you are my God;*
may your good Spirit
*   lead me on level ground.*

PSALM 143:10

The LORD is good to all;
*   he has compassion on all he has made.*

PSALM 145:9

Jesus said,
"The Spirit of the Lord is on me,
*   because he has anointed me*
*   to preach good news to the poor.*
He has sent me to proclaim freedom for the prisoners
*   and recovery of sight for the blind,*
to release the oppressed,
*   to proclaim the year of the Lord's favor."*

LUKE 4:18–19

God's Protection

If you make the Most High your dwelling—
*   even the LORD, who is my refuge—*
then no harm will befall you,
*   no disaster will come near your tent.*

PSALM 91:9–10

You are my hiding place, [O LORD];
*   you will protect me from trouble*
*   and surround me with songs of deliverance.*

PSALM 32:7

Through the victories you gave, his glory is great;
*   you have bestowed on him splendor and majesty.*
Surely you have granted him eternal blessings
*   and made him glad with the joy of your presence.*

PSALM 21:5–6

"Be strong and courageous. Do not be afraid or terrified because of them, for the LORD your God goes with you; he will never leave you nor forsake you."

DEUTERONOMY 31:6

God's Protection

Whoever dwells in the shelter of the Most High
  will rest in the shadow of the Almighty.
They say of the LORD, "He is my refuge and
    my fortress,
  my God, in whom I trust."
Surely he will save you
    from the fowler's snare
  and from the deadly pestilence.
He will cover you with his feathers,
  and under his wings you will find refuge;
  his faithfulness will be your shield and rampart.
You will not fear the terror of night,
  nor the arrow that flies by day,
nor the pestilence that stalks in the darkness,
  nor the plague that destroys at midday.
A thousand may fall at your side,
  ten thousand at your right hand,
  but it will not come near you.

PSALM 91:1 – 7 TNIV

God's Protection

No one will be able to stand up against you all the days of your life. As I was with Moses, so I will be with you; I will never leave you nor forsake you.

JOSHUA 1:5

The LORD said, "I am with you and will watch over you wherever you go, and I will bring you back to this land. I will not leave you until I have done what I have promised you."

GENESIS 28:15

Let all who take refuge in you be glad;
  let them ever sing for joy.
Spread your protection over them,
  that those who love your name may rejoice
    in you.

PSALM 5:11

The LORD loves the just
  and will not forsake his faithful ones.
They will be protected forever.

PSALM 37:28

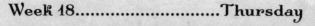

God's Protection

Fear not, for I have redeemed you;
*   I have summoned you by name; you are mine.*
When you pass through the waters,
*   I will be with you;*
and when you pass through the rivers,
*   they will not sweep over you.*
When you walk through the fire,
*   you will not be burned;*
*   the flames will not set you ablaze.*
For I am the LORD, your God.

ISAIAH 43:1–3

Jesus said, "Where two or three come together in my name, there am I with them."

MATTHEW 18:20

Jesus said, "Surely I am with you always, to the very end of the age."

MATTHEW 28:20

God's Protection

"Because they love me," says the LORD, "I will
    rescue them;
  I will protect them, for they acknowledge
    my name.
They will call on me, and I will answer them;
  I will be with them in trouble,
  I will deliver them and honor them."

PSALM 91:14–15 TNIV

It was the LORD our God himself who brought us
and our fathers up out of Egypt, from that land of
slavery, and performed those great signs before our
eyes. He protected us on our entire journey and
among all the nations through which we traveled.

JOSHUA 24:17

"Because of the oppression of the weak
    and the groaning of the needy,
I will now arise," says the LORD.
  "I will protect them from those who
    malign them."
O LORD, you will keep us safe
  and protect us from such people forever.

PSALM 12:5, 7

God's Protection

Jesus said, "Holy Father, protect them by the power of your name.... My prayer is not that you take them out of the world but that you protect them from the evil one."

JOHN 17:11, 15

The righteous may have many troubles,
*   but the LORD delivers them from them all;*
he protects all their bones,
*   not one of them will be broken.*

PSALM 34:19–20 TNIV

Blessed are those who have regard for the weak;
*   the LORD delivers them in times of trouble.*
The LORD protects and preserves them—
*   they are counted among the blessed in*
*   the land—*
*   he does not give them over to the desire of*
*   their foes.*

PSALM 41:1–2 TNIV

The Lord is faithful, and he will strengthen and protect you from the evil one.

2 THESSALONIANS 3:3

Grace

It does not, therefore, depend on human desire or effort, but on God's mercy.

ROMANS 9:16 TNIV

He ... gives grace to the humble.

PROVERBS 3:34

[God] gives us more grace. That is why Scripture says:

"God opposes the proud
but gives grace to the humble."

JAMES 4:6

By the grace of God I am what I am, and his grace to me was not without effect. No, I worked harder than all of them — yet not I, but the grace of God that was with me.

1 CORINTHIANS 15:10

The Word became flesh and made his dwelling among us. We have seen his glory, the glory of the One and Only, who came from the Father, full of grace and truth.

JOHN 1:14

Grace

Let us then approach the throne of grace with confidence, so that we may receive mercy and find grace to help us in our time of need.

HEBREWS 4:16

It is by grace you have been saved, through faith — and this not from yourselves, it is the gift of God — not by works, so that no one can boast. For we are God's workmanship, created in Christ Jesus to do good works, which God prepared in advance for us to do.

EPHESIANS 2:8–10

The law was given through Moses; grace and truth came through Jesus Christ.

JOHN 1:17

Paul and Barnabas spent considerable time [at Iconium], speaking boldly for the Lord, who confirmed the message of his grace by enabling them to do miraculous signs and wonders.

ACTS 14:3

I commit you to God and to the word of his grace, which can build you up and give you an inheritance among all those who are sanctified.

ACTS 20:32

Grace

The LORD is gracious and compassionate,
slow to anger and rich in love.

PSALM 145:8

Grace and peace be yours in abundance through the knowledge of God and of Jesus our Lord.

2 PETER 1:2

Because of his great love for us, God, who is rich in mercy, made us alive with Christ even when we were dead in transgressions — it is by grace you have been saved.

EPHESIANS 2:4–5

All have sinned and fall short of the glory of God, and are justified freely by his grace through the redemption that came by Christ Jesus.

ROMANS 3:23–24

The gift is not like the trespass. For if the many died by the trespass of the one man, how much more did God's grace and the gift that came by the grace of the one man, Jesus Christ, overflow to the many!

ROMANS 5:15

Grace

God is able to make all grace abound to you, so that
in all things at all times, having all that you need,
you will abound in every good work.

2 CORINTHIANS 9:8

You know the grace of our Lord Jesus Christ, that
though he was rich, yet for your sakes he became
poor, so that you through his poverty might
become rich.

2 CORINTHIANS 8:9

[God] has saved us and called us to a holy life — not
because of anything we have done but because of
his own purpose and grace. This grace was given us
in Christ Jesus before the beginning of time.

2 TIMOTHY 1:9

[God] saved us, not because of righteous things we
had done, but because of his mercy. He saved us
through the washing of rebirth and renewal by the
Holy Spirit, whom he poured out on us generously
through Jesus Christ our Savior, so that, having
been justified by his grace, we might become heirs
having the hope of eternal life.

TITUS 3:5–7

Grace

If, by the trespass of the one man, death reigned through that one man, how much more will those who receive God's abundant provision of grace and of the gift of righteousness reign in life through the one man, Jesus Christ.

ROMANS 5:17

Sin shall not be your master, because you are not under law, but under grace.

ROMANS 6:14

God set me apart from birth and called me by his grace.

GALATIANS 1:15

To each one of us grace has been given as Christ apportioned it. This is why it says:

"When he ascended on high,
he took many captives
and gave gifts to his people."

EPHESIANS 4:7–8 TNIV

Let your conversation be always full of grace, seasoned with salt, so that you may know how to answer everyone.

COLOSSIANS 4:6

Grace

From the fullness of his grace we have all received one blessing after another.

JOHN 1:16

[The Lord] said to me, "My grace is sufficient for you, for my power is made perfect in weakness." Therefore I will boast all the more gladly about my weaknesses, so that Christ's power may rest on me.

2 CORINTHIANS 12:9

May our Lord Jesus Christ himself and God our Father, who loved us and by his grace gave us eternal encouragement and good hope, encourage your hearts and strengthen you in every good deed and word.

2 THESSALONIANS 2:16–17

The grace of God has appeared that offers salvation to all people. It teaches us to say "No" to ungodliness and worldly passions, and to live self-controlled, upright and godly lives in this present age.

TITUS 2:11–12 TNIV

Each of you should use whatever gift you have received to serve others, as faithful stewards of God's grace in its various forms.

1 PETER 4:10 TNIV

Guidance

You guide me with your counsel,
*   and afterward you will take me into glory.*

PSALM 73:24

Teach me to do your will,
*   for you are my God;*
may your good Spirit
*   lead me on level ground.*

PSALM 143:10

Jesus said, "When he, the Spirit of truth, comes, he
will guide you into all truth. He will not speak on
his own; he will speak only what he hears, and he
will tell you what is yet to come."

JOHN 16:13

The LORD will guide you always;
*   he will satisfy your needs in a sun-scorched land*
*   and will strengthen your frame.*
You will be like a well-watered garden,
*   like a spring whose waters never fail.*

ISAIAH 58:11

Guidance

If I rise on the wings of the dawn,
*   if I settle on the far side of the sea,*
even there your hand will guide me,
*   your right hand will hold me fast.*

PSALM 139:9–10

The LORD is my shepherd, I shall not be in want.
*   He makes me lie down in green pastures,*
he leads me beside quiet waters,
*   he restores my soul.*
He guides me in paths of righteousness
*   for his name's sake.*

PSALM 23:1–3

We have not stopped praying for you and ask-
ing God to fill you with the knowledge of his will
through all spiritual wisdom and understanding.

COLOSSIANS 1:9

Jesus said, "My sheep listen to my voice; I know
them, and they follow me."

JOHN 10:27

Guidance

*In your unfailing love you will lead
    the people you have redeemed.
In your strength you will guide them
    to your holy dwelling.*

EXODUS 15:13

The LORD says,
*"I have seen their ways, but I will heal them;
    I will guide them and restore comfort to them."*

ISAIAH 57:18 TNIV

*In their hearts human beings plan their course,
    but the LORD establishes their steps.*

PROVERBS 16:9 TNIV

*Good and upright is the LORD;
    therefore he instructs sinners in his ways.
He guides the humble in what is right
    and teaches them his way.*

PSALM 25:8–9

Guidance

I guide you in the way of wisdom
and lead you along straight paths.

PROVERBS 4:11

He tends his flock like a shepherd:
He gathers the lambs in his arms
and carries them close to his heart;
he gently leads those that have young.

ISAIAH 40:11

I will give you shepherds after my own heart, who
will lead you with knowledge and understanding.

JEREMIAH 3:15

I will lead the blind by ways they have not known,
along unfamiliar paths I will guide them;
I will turn the darkness into light before them
and make the rough places smooth.
These are the things I will do;
I will not forsake them.

ISAIAH 42:16

Guidance

*I will instruct you and teach you in the way you
    should go;
    I will counsel you and watch over you.*

PSALM 32:8

*Teach me your way, O LORD,
    and I will walk in your truth;
    give me an undivided heart, that I may fear
        your name.*

PSALM 86:11

*[The captives] will neither hunger nor thirst,
    nor will the desert heat or the sun beat
        upon them.
He who has compassion on them will guide them
    and lead them beside springs of water.*

ISAIAH 49:10

Whether you turn to the right or to the left, your
ears will hear a voice behind you, saying, "This is
the way; walk in it."

ISAIAH 30:21

Guidance

Jesus said, "The sheep listen to [the shepherd's] voice. He calls his own sheep by name and leads them out. When he has brought out all his own, he goes on ahead of them, and his sheep follow him because they know his voice. But they will never follow a stranger; in fact, they will run away from him because they do not recognize a stranger's voice."

JOHN 10:3–5

They will come with weeping;
    they will pray as I bring them back.
I will lead them beside streams of water
    on a level path where they will not stumble.

JEREMIAH 31:9

This is what the LORD says—
    your Redeemer, the Holy One of Israel:
"I am the LORD your God,
    who teaches you what is best for you,
    who directs you in the way you should go."

ISAIAH 48:17

Healing

Is anyone among you sick? Let them call the elders of the church to pray over them and anoint them with oil in the name of the Lord. And the prayer offered in faith will make them well; the Lord will raise them up. If they have sinned, they will be forgiven.

JAMES 5:14–15 TNIV

Blessed are those who have regard for the weak;
*   the LORD delivers them in times of trouble.*
The LORD sustains them on their sickbed
*   and restores them from their bed of illness.*

PSALM 41:1, 3 TNIV

He himself bore our sins in his body on the tree, so that we might die to sins and live for righteousness; by his wounds you have been healed.

1 PETER 2:24

O LORD my God, I called to you for help
*   and you healed me.*
O LORD, you brought me up from the grave;
*   you spared me from going down into the pit.*

PSALM 30:2–3

Healing

Do not be wise in your own eyes;
   fear the Lord and shun evil.
This will bring health to your body
   and nourishment to your bones.

PROVERBS 3:7–8

Worship the LORD your God, and his blessing will
be on your food and water. I will take away sickness
from among you, and none will miscarry or be bar-
ren in your land. I will give you a full life span.

EXODUS 23:25–26

Heal me, O LORD, and I will be healed;
   save me and I will be saved,
   for you are the one I praise.

JEREMIAH 17:14

"I will restore you to health
   and heal your wounds,"
      declares the LORD.

JEREMIAH 30:17

Healing

[God] said, "If you listen carefully to the voice of the LORD your God and do what is right in his eyes, if you pay attention to his commands and keep all his decrees, I will not bring on you any of the diseases I brought on the Egyptians, for I am the LORD, who heals you."

EXODUS 15:26

For you who revere my name, the sun of righteousness will rise with healing in its wings. And you will go out and leap like calves released from the stall.

MALACHI 4:2

My son, pay attention to what I say;
*   turn your ear to my words.*
Do not let them out of your sight,
*   keep them within your heart;*
for they are life to those who find them
*   and health to one's whole body.*

PROVERBS 4:20–22 TNIV

He sent forth his word and healed them;
*   he rescued them from the grave.*

PSALM 107:20

Healing

Praise the LORD, O my soul,
*   and forget not all his benefits—*
who ... heals all your diseases,
who redeems your life from the pit
*   and crowns you with love and compassion,*
who satisfies your desires with good things
*   so that your youth is renewed like the eagle's.*

PSALM 103:2–5

God anointed Jesus of Nazareth with the Holy Spirit
and power, and ... he went around doing good and
healing all who were under the power of the devil,
because God was with him.

ACTS 10:38

He was pierced for our transgressions,
*   he was crushed for our iniquities;*
the punishment that brought us peace was upon him,
*   and by his wounds we are healed.*

ISAIAH 53:5

Healing

*Reckless words pierce like a sword,
    but the tongue of the wise brings healing.*

PROVERBS 12:18

Jesus went throughout Galilee, teaching in their
synagogues, preaching the good news of the kingdom, and healing every disease and sickness among
the people. News about him spread all over Syria,
and people brought to him all who were ill with
various diseases, those suffering severe pain, the
demon-possessed, those having seizures, and the
paralyzed, and he healed them.

MATTHEW 4:23–24

*A cheerful look brings joy to the heart,
    and good news gives health to the bones.*

PROVERBS 15:30

Dear friend, I pray that you may enjoy good health
and that all may go well with you, even as your soul
is getting along well.

3 JOHN 2

Healing

I will bring health and healing to [this city]; I will heal my people and will let them enjoy abundant peace and security.

JEREMIAH 33:6

Jesus said, "These signs will accompany those who believe: In my name they will ... place their hands on sick people, and they will get well."

MARK 16:17–18

Pleasant words are a honeycomb,
sweet to the soul and healing to the bones.

PROVERBS 16:24

When evening came, many who were demon-possessed were brought to him, and he drove out the spirits with a word and healed all the sick. This was to fulfill what was spoken through the prophet Isaiah:

"He took up our infirmities
and carried our diseases."

MATTHEW 8:16–17

Holiness

"I will not violate my covenant
    or alter what my lips have uttered.
Once for all, I have sworn by my holiness —
    and I will not lie to David," says the LORD.

PSALM 89:34–35

Just as he who called you is holy, so be holy in all you do; for it is written: "Be holy, because I am holy."

1 PETER 1:15–16

May [the Lord] strengthen your hearts so that you will be blameless and holy in the presence of our God and Father when our Lord Jesus comes with all his holy ones.

1 THESSALONIANS 3:13

God did not call us to be impure, but to live a holy life.

1 THESSALONIANS 4:7

The LORD has dealt with me according to
    my righteousness;
    according to the cleanness of my hands he has
    rewarded me.

PSALM 18:20

Holiness

There is no one holy like the LORD;
*   there is no one besides you;*
*   there is no Rock like our God.*

1 SAMUEL 2:2

As you come to him, the living Stone ... you also,
like living stones, are being built into a spiritual
house to be a holy priesthood, offering spiritual sacrifices acceptable to God through Jesus Christ.

1 PETER 2:4–5

He chose us in him before the creation of the world
to be holy and blameless in his sight.

EPHESIANS 1:4

You ought to live holy and godly lives as you look
forward to the day of God and speed its coming.

2 PETER 3:11–12

Since we have these promises, dear friends, let us
purify ourselves from everything that contaminates
body and spirit, perfecting holiness out of reverence
for God.

2 CORINTHIANS 7:1

Holiness

Make every effort to live in peace with everyone and to be holy; without holiness no one will see the Lord.

HEBREWS 12:14 TNIV

Once you were alienated from God and were enemies in your minds because of your evil behavior. But now he has reconciled you by Christ's physical body through death to present you holy in his sight, without blemish and free from accusation.

COLOSSIANS 1:21–22

Moses and the Israelites sang this song to the LORD:

"Who among the gods is like you, O LORD?
Who is like you—
majestic in holiness,
awesome in glory,
working wonders?"

EXODUS 15:1, 11

Ascribe to the LORD the glory due his name;
worship the LORD in the splendor of his holiness.

PSALM 29:2

Holiness

Your statutes stand firm;
*   holiness adorns your house*
*   for endless days, O LORD.*

PSALM 93:5

Worship the LORD in the splendor of his holiness;
*   tremble before him, all the earth.*

PSALM 96:9

The LORD says,
"When they see among them their children,
*   the work of my hands,*
they will keep my name holy;
*   they will acknowledge the holiness of the Holy*
One of Jacob,
*   and will stand in awe of the God of Israel."*

ISAIAH 29:23

I will show my greatness and my holiness, and I will
make myself known in the sight of many nations.
Then they will know that I am the LORD.

EZEKIEL 38:23

Holiness

God disciplines us for our good, that we may share
in his holiness. No discipline seems pleasant at the
time, but painful. Later on, however, it produces a
harvest of righteousness and peace for those who
have been trained by it.

HEBREWS 12:10–11

Women will be saved through childbearing—if
they continue in faith, love and holiness with pro-
priety.

1 TIMOTHY 2:15

I urge, then, first of all, that requests, prayers,
intercession and thanksgiving be made for everyone—for kings and all those in authority, that we
may live peaceful and quiet lives in all godliness
and holiness.

1 TIMOTHY 2:1–2

You were taught, with regard to your former way of
life, to put off your old self, which is being cor-
rupted by its deceitful desires; to be made new in
the attitude of your minds; and to put on the new
self, created to be like God in true righteousness
and holiness.

EPHESIANS 4:22–24

Holiness

It is because of him that you are in Christ Jesus, who has become for us wisdom from God — that is, our righteousness, holiness and redemption.

1 CORINTHIANS 1:30

Now that you have been set free from sin and have become slaves to God, the benefit you reap leads to holiness, and the result is eternal life.

ROMANS 6:22

Who may ascend the mountain of the LORD?
Who may stand in his holy place?
Those who have clean hands and a pure heart,
who do not put their trust in an idol
or swear by a false god.

PSALM 24:3 – 4 TNIV

Your ways, O God, are holy.
What god is so great as our God?
You are the God who performs miracles;
you display your power among the peoples.

PSALM 77:13 – 14

Holy Spirit

The Spirit helps us in our weakness. We do not know what we ought to pray for, but the Spirit himself intercedes for us with groans that words cannot express.

ROMANS 8:26

You also were included in Christ when you heard the word of truth, the gospel of your salvation. Having believed, you were marked in him with a seal, the promised Holy Spirit, who is a deposit guaranteeing our inheritance until the redemption of those who are God's possession.

EPHESIANS 1:13–14

There is now no condemnation for those who are in Christ Jesus, because through Christ Jesus the law of the Spirit of life set me free from the law of sin and death.

ROMANS 8:1–2

Jesus said, "When he, the Spirit of truth, comes, he will guide you into all truth. He will not speak on his own; he will speak only what he hears, and he will tell you what is yet to come."

JOHN 16:13

Holy Spirit

Repent and be baptized, every one of you, in the name of Jesus Christ for the forgiveness of your sins. And you will receive the gift of the Holy Spirit. The promise is for you and your children and for all who are far off—for all whom the Lord our God will call.

ACTS 2:38–39

Do not believe every spirit, but test the spirits to see whether they are from God.... This is how you can recognize the Spirit of God: Every spirit that acknowledges that Jesus Christ has come in the flesh is from God.

1 JOHN 4:1–2

In the last days, God says,
I will pour out my Spirit on all people.
Your sons and daughters will prophesy,
your young men will see visions,
your old men will dream dreams.

ACTS 2:17

He saved us through the washing of rebirth and renewal by the Holy Spirit, whom he poured out on us generously through Jesus Christ our Savior.

TITUS 3:5–6

Holy Spirit

If the Spirit of him who raised Jesus from the dead is living in you, he who raised Christ from the dead will also give life to your mortal bodies through his Spirit, who lives in you.

ROMANS 8:11

Jesus said, "I will ask the Father, and he will give you another Counselor to be with you forever — the Spirit of truth. The world cannot accept him, because it neither sees him nor knows him. But you know him, for he lives with you and will be in you."

JOHN 14:16–17

Jesus said,
"The Spirit of the Lord is on me,
    because he has anointed me
    to preach good news to the poor.
He has sent me to proclaim freedom for the prisoners
    and recovery of sight for the blind,
to release the oppressed,
    to proclaim the year of the Lord's favor."

LUKE 4:18–19

Holy Spirit

Jesus stood and said in a loud voice, "Let anyone who is thirsty come to me and drink. Whoever believes in me, as Scripture has said, rivers of living water will flow from within them." By this he meant the Spirit.

JOHN 7:37–39 TNIV

This is how the birth of Jesus Christ came about: His mother Mary was pledged to be married to Joseph, but before they came together, she was found to be with child through the Holy Spirit.

MATTHEW 1:18

John the Baptist said, "I baptize you with water for repentance. But after me will come one who is more powerful than I, whose sandals I am not fit to carry. He will baptize you with the Holy Spirit and with fire."

MATTHEW 3:11

Jesus said, "Whenever you are arrested and brought to trial, do not worry beforehand about what to say. Just say whatever is given you at the time, for it is not you speaking, but the Holy Spirit."

MARK 13:11

Holy Spirit

No one who is speaking by the Spirit of God says, "Jesus be cursed," and no one can say, "Jesus is Lord," except by the Holy Spirit.

1 CORINTHIANS 12:3

Jesus answered, "Very truly I tell you, no one can enter the kingdom of God without being born of water and the Spirit. Flesh gives birth to flesh, but the Spirit gives birth to spirit."

JOHN 3:5–6 TNIV

The kingdom of God is not a matter of eating and drinking, but of righteousness, peace and joy in the Holy Spirit.

ROMANS 14:17

John the Baptist said, "I baptize you with water, but [Jesus] will baptize you with the Holy Spirit."

MARK 1:8

Those who are led by the Spirit of God are sons of God. For you did not receive a spirit that makes you a slave again to fear, but you received the Spirit of sonship. And by him we cry, *"Abba*, Father." The Spirit himself testifies with our spirit that we are God's children.

ROMANS 8:14–16

Holy Spirit

Jesus said, "The Counselor, the Holy Spirit, whom the Father will send in my name, will teach you all things and will remind you of everything I have said to you."

JOHN 14:26

Now to each one the manifestation of the Spirit is given for the common good. To one there is given through the Spirit the message of wisdom, to another the message of knowledge by means of the same Spirit, to another faith by the same Spirit, to another gifts of healing by that one Spirit, to another miraculous powers, to another prophecy, to another distinguishing between spirits, to another speaking in different kinds of tongues, and to still another the interpretation of tongues. All these are the work of one and the same Spirit, and he gives them to each one, just as he determines.

1 CORINTHIANS 12:7–11

Do you not know that your body is a temple of the Holy Spirit, who is in you, whom you have received from God? You are not your own; you were bought at a price. Therefore honor God with your body.

1 CORINTHIANS 6:19–20

Honesty

The LORD detests lying lips,
but he delights in people who are trustworthy.

PROVERBS 12:22 TNIV

Those who walk righteously
and speak what is right,
who reject gain from extortion
and keep their hands from accepting bribes,
who stop their ears against plots of murder
and shut their eyes against contemplating evil —
they are the ones who will dwell on the heights,
whose refuge will be the mountain fortress.
Their bread will be supplied,
and water will not fail them.

ISAIAH 33:15 – 16 TNIV

Whatever is true, whatever is noble, whatever is
right, whatever is pure, whatever is lovely, whatever
is admirable — if anything is excellent or praiseworthy — think about such things.

PHILIPPIANS 4:8

Honesty

Truthful lips endure forever.

PROVERBS 12:19

The LORD God is a sun and shield;
*   the LORD bestows favor and honor;*
no good thing does he withhold
*   from those whose walk is blameless.*

PSALM 84:11

I know, my God, that you test the heart and are
pleased with integrity.

1 CHRONICLES 29:17

Vindicate me, O LORD,
*   for I have led a blameless life;*
I have trusted in the LORD
*   without wavering.*
Test me, O LORD, and try me,
*   examine my heart and my mind;*
for your love is ever before me,
*   and I walk continually in your truth.*

PSALM 26:1–3

Honesty

Jesus said, "Whoever can be trusted with very little can also be trusted with much, and whoever is dishonest with very little will also be dishonest with much."

LUKE 16:10

In my integrity you uphold me
and set me in your presence forever.

PSALM 41:12

The righteous lead blameless lives;
blessed are their children after them.

PROVERBS 20:7 TNIV

He holds victory in store for the upright,
he is a shield to those whose walk is blameless,
for he guards the course of the just
and protects the way of his faithful ones.

PROVERBS 2:7–8

Those who walk uprightly
enter into peace.

ISAIAH 57:2

Honesty

Whoever of you loves life
and desires to see many good days,
keep your tongue from evil
and your lips from speaking lies.

PSALM 34:12–13

When the LORD takes pleasure in anyone's way,
he causes their enemies to make peace with them.

PROVERBS 16:7 TNIV

A truthful witness gives honest testimony.

PROVERBS 12:17

The integrity of the upright guides them,
but the unfaithful are destroyed by
their duplicity.

PROVERBS 11:3

Love ... rejoices with the truth.

1 CORINTHIANS 13:6

Honesty

An honest answer
is like a kiss on the lips.

PROVERBS 24:26

Whoever walks in integrity walks securely,
but whoever takes crooked paths will be
found out.

PROVERBS 10:9 TNIV

Stand firm then, with the belt of truth buckled
around your waist, with the breastplate of righteousness in place.

EPHESIANS 6:14

Surely you desire truth in the inner parts;
you teach me wisdom in the inmost place.

PSALM 51:6

The righteous hate what is false,
but the wicked bring shame and disgrace.

PROVERBS 13:5

Honesty

Those who walk righteously
and speak what is right...
they are the ones who will dwell on the heights,
whose refuge will be the mountain fortress.
Their bread will be supplied,
and water will not fail them.

ISAIAH 33:15–16 TNIV

Righteousness guards the person of integrity.

PROVERBS 13:6 TNIV

Those whose walk is blameless,
who do what is righteous,
who speak the truth from their hearts ...
Whoever does these things
will never be shaken.

PSALM 15:2, 5 TNIV

Kings take pleasure in honest lips;
they value persons who speak what is right.

PROVERBS 16:13 TNIV

Hopes and Dreams

No one whose hope is in you
 will ever be put to shame.

PSALM 25:3

The prospect of the righteous is joy,
 but the hopes of the wicked come to nothing.

PROVERBS 10:28

Those who hope in the LORD
 will renew their strength.
They will soar on wings like eagles;
 they will run and not grow weary,
 they will walk and not be faint.

ISAIAH 40:31

Know also that wisdom is sweet to your soul;
 if you find it, there is a future hope for you,
 and your hope will not be cut off.

PROVERBS 24:14

Hopes and Dreams

[Love] ... always hopes.

1 CORINTHIANS 13:7

The needy will not always be forgotten,
nor the hope of the afflicted ever perish.

PSALM 9:18

We rejoice in the hope of the glory of God. Not only so, but we also rejoice in our sufferings, because we know that suffering produces perseverance; perseverance, character; and character, hope. And hope does not disappoint us, because God has poured out his love into our hearts by the Holy Spirit, whom he has given us.

ROMANS 5:2–5

A horse is a vain hope for deliverance;
despite all its great strength it cannot save.
But the eyes of the LORD are on those who fear him,
on those whose hope is in his unfailing love,
to deliver them from death
and keep them alive in famine.

PSALM 33:17–19

Hopes and Dreams

We have put our hope in the living God, who is the Savior of all people, and especially of those who believe.

1 TIMOTHY 4:10 TNIV

May the God of hope fill you with all joy and peace as you trust in him, so that you may overflow with hope by the power of the Holy Spirit.

ROMANS 15:13

Now to him who is able to do immeasurably more than all we ask or imagine, according to his power that is at work within us, to him be glory in the church and in Christ Jesus throughout all generations, for ever and ever! Amen.

EPHESIANS 3:20–21

In the morning, O LORD, you hear my voice;
*   in the morning I lay my requests before you*
*   and wait in expectation.*

PSALM 5:3

Set your hope fully on the grace to be given you when Jesus Christ is revealed.

1 PETER 1:13

Hopes and Dreams

When the LORD restored the fortunes of Zion,
*   we were like those who dreamed.*
Our mouths were filled with laughter,
*   our tongues with songs of joy.*
Then it was said among the nations,
*   "The LORD has done great things for them."*

PSALM 126:1–2 TNIV

I will pour out my Spirit on all people.
Your sons and daughters will prophesy,
*   your old men will dream dreams,*
*   your young men will see visions.*
Even on my servants, both men and women,
*   I will pour out my Spirit in those days.*

JOEL 2:28–29

"I know the plans I have for you," declares the
LORD, "plans to prosper you and not to harm you,
plans to give you hope and a future."

JEREMIAH 29:11

Hopes and Dreams

*"No eye has seen,
no ear has heard,
no mind has conceived
what God has prepared for those who
love him"*—
but God has revealed it to us by his Spirit.

1 CORINTHIANS 2:9–10

Listen, you who say, "Today or tomorrow we will go to this or that city, spend a year there, carry on business and make money. "Why, you do not even know what will happen tomorrow. What is your life? You are a mist that appears for a little while and then vanishes. Instead, you ought to say, "If it is the Lord's will, we will live and do this or that."

JAMES 4:13–15

I am convinced that ... neither the present nor the future, nor any powers, neither height nor depth, nor anything else in all creation, will be able to separate us from the love of God that is in Christ Jesus our Lord.

ROMANS 8:38–39

Hopes and Dreams

Sustain me according to your promise, and I
will live;
do not let my hopes be dashed.

PSALM 119:116

Hope that is seen is no hope at all. Who hopes for
what they already have? But if we hope for what we
do not yet have, we wait for it patiently.

ROMANS 8:24–25 TNIV

Against all hope, Abraham in hope believed and
so became the father of many nations.... Without
weakening in his faith, he faced the fact that his
body was as good as dead—since he was about a
hundred years old—and that Sarah's womb was
also dead. Yet he did not waver through unbelief
regarding the promise of God, but was strengthened
in his faith and gave glory to God, being fully persuaded that God had power to do what he
had promised.

ROMANS 4:18–21

The LORD says, "Call to me and I will answer you
and tell you great and unsearchable things you do
not know."

JEREMIAH 33:3

Jesus Christ

To us a child is born,
to us a son is given,
and the government will be on his shoulders.
And he will be called
Wonderful Counselor, Mighty God,
Everlasting Father, Prince of Peace.
Of the increase of his government and peace
there will be no end.

ISAIAH 9:6-7

An angel of the Lord appeared to [Joseph] in a dream and said, "Joseph son of David, do not be afraid to take Mary home as your wife, because what is conceived in her is from the Holy Spirit. She will give birth to a son, and you are to give him the name Jesus, because he will save his people from their sins."

MATTHEW 1:20-21

As soon as Jesus was baptized, he went up out of the water. At that moment heaven was opened, and he saw the Spirit of God descending like a dove and lighting on him. And a voice from heaven said, "This is my Son, whom I love; with him I am well pleased."

MATTHEW 3:16-17

Jesus Christ

If you confess with your mouth, "Jesus is Lord," and believe in your heart that God raised him from the dead, you will be saved.

ROMANS 10:9

God exalted him to the highest place
    and gave him the name that is above
        every name,
that at the name of Jesus every knee should bow,
    in heaven and on earth and under the earth,
and every tongue confess that Jesus Christ is Lord,
    to the glory of God the Father.

PHILIPPIANS 2:9–11

Since we have a great high priest who has gone through the heavens, Jesus the Son of God, let us hold firmly to the faith we profess. For we do not have a high priest who is unable to sympathize with our weaknesses, but we have one who has been tempted in every way, just as we are—yet was without sin.

HEBREWS 4:14–15

Let us fix our eyes on Jesus, the author and perfecter of our faith.

HEBREWS 12:2

Jesus Christ

Jesus said, "God so loved the world that he gave his one and only Son, that whoever believes in him shall not perish but have eternal life. For God did not send his Son into the world to condemn the world, but to save the world through him."

JOHN 3:16–17

Jesus said, "Here I am! I stand at the door and knock. If anyone hears my voice and opens the door, I will come in and eat with them, and they with me."

REVELATION 3:20 TNIV

God anointed Jesus of Nazareth with the Holy Spirit and power, and how he went around doing good and healing all who were under the power of the devil, because God was with him.

ACTS 10:38

Jesus Christ is the same yesterday and today and forever.

HEBREWS 13:8

Jesus answered, "I am the way and the truth and the life. No one comes to the Father except through me."

JOHN 14:6

Jesus Christ

Here is a trustworthy saying that deserves full acceptance: Christ Jesus came into the world to save sinners.

1 TIMOTHY 1:15

If anyone acknowledges that Jesus is the Son of God, God lives in them and they in God.

1 JOHN 4:15 TNIV

Jesus asked, "Who do you say I am?" Simon Peter answered, "You are the Messiah, the Son of the living God." Jesus replied, "Blessed are you, Simon son of Jonah, for this was not revealed to you by flesh and blood, but by my Father in heaven."

MATTHEW 16:15–17 TNIV

God made him who had no sin to be sin for us, so that in him we might become the righteousness of God.

2 CORINTHIANS 5:21

Jesus said, "I am the light of the world. Whoever follows me will never walk in darkness, but will have the light of life."

JOHN 8:12

Jesus Christ

Christ redeemed us from the curse of the law by becoming a curse for us, for it is written: "Cursed is everyone who is hung on a tree." He redeemed us in order that the blessing given to Abraham might come to the Gentiles through Christ Jesus, so that by faith we might receive the promise of the Spirit.

GALATIANS 3:13–14

Thanks be to God! He gives us the victory through our Lord Jesus Christ.

1 CORINTHIANS 15:57

There is one God and one mediator between God and human beings, Christ Jesus, himself human, who gave himself as a ransom for all people.

1 TIMOTHY 2:5–6 TNIV

This grace was given us in Christ Jesus before the beginning of time, but it has now been revealed through the appearing of our Savior, Christ Jesus, who has destroyed death and has brought life and immortality to light through the gospel.

2 TIMOTHY 1:9–10

Everyone who believes that Jesus is the Christ is born of God.

1 JOHN 5:1

Jesus Christ

God raised us up with Christ and seated us with him in the heavenly realms in Christ Jesus.

EPHESIANS 2:6

We wait for the blessed hope — the glorious appearing of our great God and Savior, Jesus Christ, who gave himself for us to redeem us from all wickedness and to purify for himself a people that are his very own, eager to do what is good.

TITUS 2:13–14

Who is it that overcomes the world? Only the one who believes that Jesus is the Son of God.

1 JOHN 5:5 TNIV

This is how you can recognize the Spirit of God: Every spirit that acknowledges that Jesus Christ has come in the flesh is from God, but every spirit that does not acknowledge Jesus is not from God. This is the spirit of the antichrist, which you have heard is coming and even now is already in the world.

1 JOHN 4:2–3

This is how we know what love is: Jesus Christ laid down his life for us.

1 JOHN 3:16

Joy

You love righteousness and hate wickedness;
therefore God, your God, has set you above
your companions
by anointing you with the oil of joy.

PSALM 45:7

Light is shed upon the righteous
and joy on the upright in heart.

PSALM 97:11

Consider it pure joy, my brothers and sisters,
whenever you face trails of many kinds, because you
know that the testing of your faith produces perseverance.

JAMES 1:2–3 TNIV

Splendor and majesty are before [the LORD];
strength and joy in his dwelling place.

1 CHRONICLES 16:27

The LORD your God will bless you in all your harvest and in all the work of your hands, and your joy
will be complete.

DEUTERONOMY 16:15

Joy

Surely you have granted [the king] eternal blessings
    and made him glad with the joy of your presence.
PSALM 21:6

You have made known to me the path of life;
    you will fill me with joy in your presence,
    with eternal pleasures at your right hand.
PSALM 16:11

Tremble before him, all the earth!
    The world is firmly established; it cannot
      be moved.
Let the heavens rejoice, let the earth be glad;
    let them say among the nations, "The
      LORD reigns!"
Let the sea resound, and all that is in it;
    let the fields be jubilant, and everything in them!
Then the trees of the forest will sing,
    they will sing for joy before the LORD,
    for he comes to judge the earth.
1 CHRONICLES 16:30–33

Joy

The humble will rejoice in the LORD;
*   the needy will rejoice in the Holy One of Israel.*

ISAIAH 29:19

The joy of the LORD is your strength.

NEHEMIAH 8:10

Jesus said, "Until now you have not asked for any-thing in my name. Ask and you will receive, and your joy will be complete."

JOHN 16:24

Though you have not seen [Jesus], you love him; and even though you do not see him now, you believe in him and are filled with an inexpressible and glori-ous joy, for you are receiving the goal of your faith, the salvation of your souls.

1 PETER 1:8–9

Those who sow in tears
*   will reap with songs of joy.*

PSALM 126:5

Joy

You turned my wailing into dancing;
*   you removed my sackcloth and clothed me*
*   with joy,*
that my heart may sing to you and not be silent.
*   O Lord my God, I will give you thanks forever.*

PSALM 30:11–12

[God] will yet fill your mouth with laughter
*   and your lips with shouts of joy.*

JOB 8:21

The Lord is my strength and my shield;
*   my heart trusts in him, and I am helped.*
My heart leaps for joy
*   and I will give thanks to him in song.*

PSALM 28:7

Restore to me the joy of your salvation
*   and grant me a willing spirit, to sustain me.*

PSALM 51:12

Joy

Clap your hands, all you nations;
shout to God with cries of joy.
God has ascended amid shouts of joy,
the LORD amid the sounding of trumpets.

PSALM 47:1, 5

Let all who take refuge in you be glad, [O LORD];
let them ever sing for joy.

PSALM 5:11

You make me glad by your deeds, O LORD;
I sing for joy at the works of your hands.

PSALM 92:4

The precepts of the LORD are right,
giving joy to the heart.

PSALM 19:8

When anxiety was great within me,
your consolation brought joy to my soul.

PSALM 94:19

Joy

Your statutes are my heritage forever, [O LORD];
  they are the joy of my heart.

PSALM 119:111

The LORD declares,
"You will go out in joy
  and be led forth in peace;
the mountains and hills
  will burst into song before you,
and all the trees of the field
  will clap their hands."

ISAIAH 55:12

Shouts of joy and victory
  resound in the tents of the righteous:
"The LORD'S right hand has done mighty things!"

PSALM 118:15

The prospect of the righteous is joy.

PROVERBS 10:28

Kindness

The LORD is gracious and righteous;
    our God is full of compassion.
The LORD protects the simplehearted;
    when I was in great need, he saved me.

PSALM 116:5–6

You, O Lord, are a compassionate and
      gracious God,
    slow to anger, abounding in love
      and faithfulness.

PSALM 86:15

The LORD is good to all;
    he has compassion on all he has made.

PSALM 145:9

"Though the mountains be shaken
    and the hills be removed,
yet my unfailing love for you will not be shaken
    nor my covenant of peace be removed,"
    says the LORD, who has compassion on you.

ISAIAH 54:10

Kindness

The LORD longs to be gracious to you;
*   he rises to show you compassion.*
For the LORD is a God of justice.
*   Blessed are all who wait for him!*

ISAIAH 30:18

Your compassion is great, O LORD;
*   preserve my life according to your laws.*

PSALM 119:156

As a father has compassion on his children,
*   so the LORD has compassion on those who*
*   fear him.*

PSALM 103:13

In a surge of anger
*   I hid my face from you for a moment,*
but with everlasting kindness
*   I will have compassion on you,"*
*   says the LORD your Redeemer.*

ISAIAH 54:8

Kindness

"*I will betroth you to me forever;*
I will betroth you in righteousness and justice,
in love and compassion,"
declares the LORD.

HOSEA 2:19

Because of the LORD's *great love we are not con-*
sumed,
for his compassions never fail.
They are new every morning;
great is your faithfulness.

LAMENTATIONS 3:22–23

You will again have compassion on us;
you will tread our sins underfoot
and hurl all our iniquities into the depths of
the sea.

MICAH 7:19

Even in darkness light dawns for the upright,
for those who are gracious and compassionate
and righteous.

PSALM 112:4 TNIV

Kindness

Those who are kind to the poor lend to the LORD,
*   and he will reward them for what they*
*   have done.*

PROVERBS 19:17 TNIV

Those who are kind benefit themselves,
*   but the cruel bring ruin on themselves.*

PROVERBS 11:17 TNIV

When the kindness and love of God our Savior appeared, he saved us, not because of righteous things
we had done, but because of his mercy.

TITUS 3:4–5

Whoever is kind to the needy honors God.

PROVERBS 14:31

I led them with cords of human kindness,
*   with ties of love;*
I lifted the yoke from their neck
*   and bent down to feed them.*

HOSEA 11:4

Kindness

I will tell of the kindnesses of the LORD,
*   the deeds for which he is to be praised,*
*   according to all the LORD has done for us—*
yes, the many good things he has done
*   for the house of Israel,*
*   according to his compassion and many*
*   kindnesses.*

ISAIAH 63:7

A kindhearted woman gains respect,
*   but ruthless men gain only wealth.*

PROVERBS 11:16

Anxiety weighs down the heart,
*   but a kind word cheers it up.*

PROVERBS 12:25 TNIV

As God's chosen people, holy and dearly loved,
clothe yourselves with compassion, kindness, humility, gentleness and patience.

COLOSSIANS 3:12

Kindness

"Let those who boast boast about this:
that they understand and know me,
that I am the LORD, who exercises kindness,
justice and righteousness on earth,
for in these I delight,"
declares the LORD.

JEREMIAH 9:24 TNIV

Whoever increases wealth by taking interest or profit
from the poor
amasses it for another, who will be kind to
the poor.

PROVERBS 28:8 TNIV

God's kindness leads you toward repentance.

ROMANS 2:4

[The living God] has shown kindness by giving you rain from heaven and crops in their seasons; he provides you with plenty of food and fills your hearts with joy.

ACTS 14:17

Love

I pray that you, being rooted and established in love, may have power, together with all the saints, to grasp how wide and long and high and deep is the love of Christ, and to know this love that surpasses knowledge—that you may be filled to the measure of all the fullness of God.

EPHESIANS 3:17–19

If you really keep the royal law found in Scripture, "Love your neighbor as yourself," you are doing right.

JAMES 2:8

We love because he first loved us.

1 JOHN 4:19

Jesus said, "Love your enemies, do good to them, and lend to them without expecting to get anything back. Then your reward will be great, and you will be sons of the Most High."

LUKE 6:35

Above all, love each other deeply, because love covers over a multitude of sins.

1 PETER 4:8

Love

No one has ever seen God; but if we love one another, God lives in us and his love is made complete in us.

1 JOHN 4:12

Love the LORD your God with all your heart and with all your soul and with all your strength.

DEUTERONOMY 6:5

If anyone acknowledges that Jesus is the Son of God, God lives in them and they in God. And so we know and rely on the love God has for us. God is love. Whoever lives in love lives in God, and God in them.

1 JOHN 4:15–16 TNIV

Because of his great love for us, God, who is rich in mercy, made us alive with Christ even when we were dead in transgressions—it is by grace you have been saved.

EPHESIANS 2:4–5

Jesus replied, "Anyone who loves me will obey my teaching. My Father will love them, and we will come to them and make our home with them."

JOHN 14:23 TNIV

Love

The LORD appeared to us in the past, saying:
"I have loved you with an everlasting love;
*   I have drawn you with loving-kindness."*

JEREMIAH 31:3

Love is patient, love is kind. It does not envy, it does not boast, it is not proud. It is not rude, it is not self-seeking, it is not easily angered, it keeps no record of wrongs. Love does not delight in evil but rejoices with the truth. It always protects, always trusts, always hopes, always perseveres. Love never fails.

1 CORINTHIANS 13:4–8

Many are the woes of the wicked,
*   but the LORD's unfailing love*
*   surrounds those who trust in him.*

PSALM 32:10 TNIV

I am convinced that neither death nor life, neither angels nor demons, neither the present nor the future, nor any powers, neither height nor depth, nor anything else in all creation, will be able to separate us from the love of God that is in Christ Jesus our Lord.

ROMANS 8:38–39

Love

This is love: not that we loved God, but that he loved us and sent his Son as an atoning sacrifice for our sins.

1 JOHN 4:10

How great is the love the Father has lavished on us, that we should be called children of God! And that is what we are!

1 JOHN 3:1

As high as the heavens are above the earth,
so great is [God's] love for those who fear him.

PSALM 103:11

Dear friends, let us love one another, for love comes from God. Everyone who loves has been born of God and knows God.

1 JOHN 4:7

God is love. Whoever lives in love lives in God, and God in him. In this way, love is made complete among us so that we will have confidence on the day of judgment, because in this world we are like him.

1 JOHN 4:16–17

Love

In your unfailing love, [LORD], you will lead
   the people you have redeemed.
In your strength you will guide them
   to your holy dwelling.

EXODUS 15:13

[The LORD] passed in front of Moses, proclaim-
ing, "The LORD, the LORD, the compassionate and
gracious God, slow to anger, abounding in love and
faithfulness, maintaining love to thousands, and
forgiving wickedness, rebellion and sin."

EXODUS 34:6–7

The Lord your God is God of gods and Lord of
lords, the great God, mighty and awesome, who
shows no partiality and accepts no bribes. He de-
fends the cause of the fatherless and the widow, and
loves the foreigners residing among you, giving them
food and clothing.

DEUTERONOMY 10:17–18 TNIV

From everlasting to everlasting
   the LORD's love is with those who fear him,
   and his righteousness with their
      children's children.

PSALM 103:17

Love

These three remain: faith, hope and love. But the greatest of these is love.

1 CORINTHIANS 13:13

The LORD set his affection on your forefathers and loved them, and he chose you, their descendants, above all the nations.

DEUTERONOMY 10:15

Surely goodness and love will follow me
all the days of my life,
and I will dwell in the house of the LORD
forever.

PSALM 23:6

I will be glad and rejoice in your love,
for you saw my affliction
and knew the anguish of my soul.

PSALM 31:7

The LORD loves righteousness and justice;
the earth is full of his unfailing love.

PSALM 33:5

Marriage

The LORD God said, "It is not good for the man to be alone. I will make a helper suitable for him." ... The LORD God caused the man to fall into a deep sleep; and while he was sleeping, he took one of the man's ribs and closed up the place with flesh. Then the LORD God made a woman from the rib he had taken out of the man, and he brought her to the man. The man said,

"This is now bone of my bones
*   and flesh of my flesh;*
she shall be called 'woman,'
*   for she was taken out of man."*
The man and his wife were both naked, and they felt
*   no shame.*

GENESIS 2:18, 21–23, 25

Marriage should be honored by all, and the marriage bed kept pure.

HEBREWS 13:4

Blessed are all who fear the LORD,
*   who walk in his ways....*
Your wife will be like a fruitful vine
*   within your house.*

PSALM 128:1, 3

Marriage

A wife of noble character is her husband's crown,
but a disgraceful wife is like decay in his bones.

PROVERBS 12:4

Wives, submit to your husbands as to the Lord.
For the husband is the head of the wife as Christ
is the head of the church, his body, of which he is
the Savior. Now as the church submits to Christ,
so also wives should submit to their husbands in
everything. Husbands, love your wives, just as
Christ loved the church and gave himself up for
her to make her holy, cleansing her by the washing
with water through the word, and to present her to
himself as a radiant church, without stain or wrinkle
or any other blemish, but holy and blameless. In
this same way, husbands ought to love their wives
as their own bodies. He who loves his wife loves
himself. After all, no one ever hated his own body,
but he feeds and cares for it, just as Christ does the
church—for we are members of his body. "For this
reason a man will leave his father and mother and
be united to his wife, and the two will become one
flesh."

EPHESIANS 5:22–31

Marriage

Encourage one another and build each other up.

1 THESSALONIANS 5:11

A wife of noble character who can find?
She is worth far more than rubies.
Her husband has full confidence in her
and lacks nothing of value.
She brings him good, not harm,
all the days of her life....
Her husband is respected at the city gate,
where he takes his seat among the elders of
the land....
Her children arise and call her blessed;
her husband also, and he praises her:
"Many women do noble things,
but you surpass them all."
Charm is deceptive, and beauty is fleeting;
but a woman who fears the LORD is to be praised.
Give her the reward she has earned,
and let her works bring her praise at the
city gate.

PROVERBS 31:10–12, 23, 28–31

Marriage

Wives, submit to your husbands, as is fitting in
the Lord.

COLOSSIANS 3:18

Houses and wealth are inherited from parents,
but a prudent wife is from the LORD.

PROVERBS 19:14

He who finds a wife finds what is good
and receives favor from the LORD.

PROVERBS 18:22

Love is patient, love is kind. It does not envy, it does
not boast, it is not proud. It is not rude, it is not self-
seeking, it is not easily angered, it keeps no record
of wrongs. Love does not delight in evil but rejoices
with the truth. It always protects, always trusts,
always hopes, always perseveres. Love never fails.

1 CORINTHIANS 13:4–8

Many waters cannot quench love;
rivers cannot wash it away.

SONG OF SONGS 8:7

Marriage

Wives are to be women worthy of respect, not malicious talkers but temperate and trustworthy in everything.

1 TIMOTHY 3:11

Drink water from your own cistern,
running water from your own well.
Should your springs overflow in the streets,
your streams of water in the public squares?
Let them be yours alone,
never to be shared with strangers.
May your fountain be blessed,
and may you rejoice in the wife of your youth.
A loving doe, a graceful deer—
may her breasts satisfy you always,
may you ever be captivated by her love.

PROVERBS 5:15–19

I belong to my lover,
and his desire is for me.

SONG OF SONGS 7:10

Marriage

If a woman has a husband who is not a believer and he is willing to live with her, she must not divorce him. For the unbelieving husband has been sanctified through his wife, and the unbelieving wife has been sanctified through her believing husband.

1 CORINTHIANS 7:13–14

Wives ... be submissive to your husbands so that, if any of them do not believe the word, they may be won over without words by the behavior of their wives, when they see the purity and reverence of your lives.

1 PETER 3:1–2

How good and pleasant it is
  when God's people live together in unity!
For there the LORD bestows his blessing,
  even life forevermore.

PSALM 133:1, 3 TNIV

Let your conversation be always full of grace.

COLOSSIANS 4:6

Money Matters

For your sakes [Christ] became poor, so that you through his poverty might become rich.

2 CORINTHIANS 8:9

My God will meet all your needs according to his glorious riches in Christ Jesus.

PHILIPPIANS 4:19

"Bring the whole tithe into the storehouse, that there may be food in my house. Test me in this," says the LORD Almighty, "and see if I will not throw open the floodgates of heaven and pour out so much blessing that you will not have room enough for it."

MALACHI 3:10

*Good people leave an inheritance for their
    children's children,
  but a sinner's wealth is stored up for
    the righteous.*

PROVERBS 13:22 TNIV

No one can serve two masters. Either you will hate the one and love the other, or you will be devoted to the one and despise the other. You cannot serve both God and Money.

MATTHEW 6:24 TNIV

Money Matters

Whoever trusts in his riches will fall,
*   but the righteous will thrive like a green leaf.*

PROVERBS 11:28

Jesus said, "Go, sell everything you have and give to the poor, and you will have treasure in heaven."

MARK 10:21

Keep your lives free from the love of money and be content with what you have, because God has said,

"Never will I leave you;
*   never will I forsake you."*

HEBREWS 13:5

Let no debt remain outstanding, except the continuing debt to love one another, for whoever loves others has fulfilled the law.

ROMANS 13:8 TNIV

Jesus said, "Give, and it will be given to you. A good measure, pressed down, shaken together and running over, will be poured into your lap. For with the measure you use, it will be measured to you."

LUKE 6:38

Money Matters

Jesus said, "[The kingdom of heaven] will be like a man going on a journey, who called his servants and entrusted his property to them. To one he gave five talents of money, to another two talents, and to another one talent, each according to his ability. Then he went on his journey. The man who had received the five talents went at once and put his money to work and gained five more.... After a long time the master of those servants returned and settled accounts with them. The man who had received the five talents brought the other five. 'Master,' he said, 'you entrusted me with five talents. See, I have gained five more.' His master replied, 'Well done, good and faithful servant! You have been faithful with a few things; I will put you in charge of many things. Come and share your master's happiness!'"

MATTHEW 25:14–16, 19–21

Dishonest money dwindles away,
but whoever gathers money little by little makes
it grow.

PROVERBS 13:11 TNIV

It is [the LORD your God] who gives you the ability to produce wealth.

DEUTERONOMY 8:18

Money Matters

Godliness with contentment is great gain. For we brought nothing into the world, and we can take nothing out of it. But if we have food and clothing, we will be content with that.

1 TIMOTHY 6:6–8

Honor the LORD with your wealth,
*   with the firstfruits of all your crops;*
then your barns will be filled to overflowing,
*   and your vats will brim over with new wine.*

PROVERBS 3:9–10

LORD, who may dwell in your sanctuary?
*   Who may live on your holy mountain?*
Those ... who lend money to the poor
*   without interest*
*   and do not accept bribes against the innocent.*
Whoever does these things
*   will never be shaken.*

PSALM 15:1–2, 5 TNIV

Money Matters

Solomon prayed, "O LORD my God ... give your
servant a discerning heart to govern your people
and to distinguish between right and wrong. For who
is able to govern this great people of yours?" The
LORD was pleased that Solomon had asked for this.
So God said to him, "Since you have asked for this
and not for long life or wealth for yourself, nor have
asked for the death of your enemies but for discern-
ment in administering justice, I will do what you
have asked. I will give you a wise and discerning
heart, so that there will never have been anyone like
you, nor will there ever be. Moreover, I will give you
what you have not asked for—both riches
and honor."

1 KINGS 3:7, 9–13

Command those who are rich in this present world
not to be arrogant nor to put their hope in wealth,
which is so uncertain, but to put their hope in God,
who richly provides us with everything for
our enjoyment.

1 TIMOTHY 6:17

Money Matters

*Blessed are those who fear the L*ORD,
who find great delight in his commands.
Their children will be mighty in the land;
the generation of the upright will be blessed.
Wealth and riches are in their houses,
and their righteousness endures forever.

PSALM 112:1–3 TNIV

I, [wisdom], love those who love me,
and those who seek me find me.
With me are riches and honor,
enduring wealth and prosperity.
My fruit is better than fine gold;
what I yield surpasses choice silver.
I walk in the way of righteousness,
along the paths of justice,
bestowing wealth on those who love me
and making their treasuries full.

PROVERBS 8:17–21

Humility and the fear of the Lord
bring wealth and honor and life.

PROVERBS 22:4

Perseverance

Be joyful in hope, patient in affliction, faithful
in prayer.

ROMANS 12:12

The end of a matter is better than its beginning,
and patience is better than pride.

ECCLESIASTES 7:8

If we hope for what we do not yet have, we wait for
it patiently.

ROMANS 8:25

Be patient, then ... until the Lord's coming. See
how the farmer waits for the land to yield its valu-
able crop and how patient he is for the autumn and
spring rains. You too, be patient and stand firm,
because the Lord's coming is near.

JAMES 5:7–8

We pray this in order that you may live a life worthy
of the Lord and may please him in every way: bearing fruit in every good work, growing in the knowledge of God, being strengthened with all power
according to his glorious might so that you may have
great endurance and patience.

COLOSSIANS 1:10–11

Perseverance

Through patience a ruler can be persuaded,
and a gentle tongue can break a bone.

PROVERBS 25:15

Those who are patient have great understanding,
but the quick-tempered display folly.

PROVERBS 14:29 TNIV

The Lord is not slow in keeping his promise, as some understand slowness. He is patient with you, not wanting anyone to perish, but everyone to come to repentance.

2 PETER 3:9

A person's wisdom yields patience;
it is to one's glory to overlook an offense.

PROVERBS 19:11 TNIV

As God's chosen people, holy and dearly loved, clothe yourselves with compassion, kindness, humility, gentleness and patience.

COLOSSIANS 3:12

Perseverance

Preach the Word; be prepared in season and out of season; correct, rebuke and encourage—with great patience and careful instruction.

2 TIMOTHY 4:2

We do not want you to become lazy, but to imitate those who through faith and patience inherit what has been promised.

HEBREWS 6:12

A hot-tempered man stirs up dissension,
but a patient man calms a quarrel.

PROVERBS 15:18

Watch your life and doctrine closely. Persevere in them, because if you do, you will save both yourself and your hearers.

1 TIMOTHY 4:16

Do not throw away your confidence; it will be richly rewarded. You need to persevere so that when you have done the will of God, you will receive what he has promised.

HEBREWS 10:35–36

Perseverance

Blessed are those who persevere under trial, because when they have stood the test, they will receive the crown of life that God has promised to those who love him.

JAMES 1:12 TNIV

We ... rejoice in our sufferings, because we know that suffering produces perseverance; perseverance, character; and character, hope.

ROMANS 5:3–4

The testing of your faith produces perseverance. Let perseverance finish its work so that you may be mature and complete, not lacking anything.

JAMES 1:3–4 TNIV

We consider blessed those who have persevered. You have heard of Job's perseverance and have seen what the Lord finally brought about. The Lord is full of compassion and mercy.

JAMES 5:11

Let us not become weary in doing good, for at the proper time we will reap a harvest if we do not give up.

GALATIANS 6:9

Perseverance

The God of all grace, who called you to his eternal glory in Christ, after you have suffered a little while, will himself restore you and make you strong, firm and steadfast.

1 PETER 5:10

Jesus said, "He who stands firm to the end will be saved."

MATTHEW 10:22

Truthful lips endure forever,
    but a lying tongue lasts only a moment.

PROVERBS 12:19

When we are cursed, we bless; when we are persecuted, we endure it; when we are slandered, we answer kindly.

1 CORINTHIANS 4:12–13

Be strong in the grace that is in Christ Jesus.... Endure hardship with us like a good soldier of Christ Jesus.

2 TIMOTHY 2:1, 3

Perseverance

Not that I have already obtained all this, or have already been made perfect, but I press on to take hold of that for which Christ Jesus took hold of me.... I do not consider myself yet to have taken hold of it. But one thing I do: Forgetting what is behind and straining toward what is ahead, I press on toward the goal to win the prize for which God has called me heavenward in Christ Jesus.

PHILIPPIANS 3:12–14

Here is a trustworthy saying:

If we died with him,
    we will also live with him;
if we endure,
    we will also reign with him.

2 TIMOTHY 2:11–12

Let us not become weary in doing good, for at the proper time we will reap a harvest if we do not give up.

GALATIANS 6:9

Jesus told his disciples a parable to show them that they should always pray and not give up.

LUKE 18:1

Peace

I will lie down and sleep in peace,
*   for you alone, O LORD,*
*   make me dwell in safety.*

PSALM 4:8

The LORD gives strength to his people;
*   the LORD blesses his people with peace.*

PSALM 29:11

The meek will inherit the land
*   and enjoy great peace.*

PSALM 37:11

Consider the blameless, observe the upright;
*   a future awaits those who seek peace.*

PSALM 37:37 TNIV

I will listen to what God the LORD will say;
*   he promises peace to his people, his saints.*

PSALM 85:8

Peace

Love and faithfulness meet together;
*   righteousness and peace kiss each other.*

PSALM 85:10

Great peace have they who love your law,
*   and nothing can make them stumble.*

PSALM 119:165

Blessed are those who find wisdom,
*   those who gain understanding. . . .*
Her ways are pleasant ways,
*   and all her paths are peace.*

PROVERBS 3:13, 17 TNIV

There is deceit in the hearts of those who plot evil,
*   but joy for those who promote peace.*

PROVERBS 12:20

A heart at peace gives life to the body,
*   but envy rots the bones.*

PROVERBS 14:30

Peace

Better a dry crust with peace and quiet
than a house full of feasting, with strife.

PROVERBS 17:1

Discipline your son, and he will give you peace;
he will bring delight to your soul.

PROVERBS 29:17

To us a child is born,
to us a son is given....
And he will be called ...
Prince of Peace.

ISAIAH 9:6

You will keep in perfect peace
those whose minds are steadfast,
because they trust in you.

ISAIAH 26:3 TNIV

When the LORD takes pleasure in anyone's way,
    he causes their enemies to make peace with them.

PROVERBS 16:7 TNIV

The fruit of righteousness will be peace;
    the effect of righteousness will be quietness and
        confidence forever.
My people will live in peaceful dwelling places,
    in secure homes,
        in undisturbed places of rest.

ISAIAH 32:17–18

How beautiful on the mountains
    are the feet of those who bring good news,
who proclaim peace.

ISAIAH 52:7

He was pierced for our transgressions,
    he was crushed for our iniquities;
the punishment that brought us peace was upon him,
    and by his wounds we are healed.

ISAIAH 53:5

Peace

"Though the mountains be shaken
*   and the hills be removed,*
yet my unfailing love for you will not be shaken
*   nor my covenant of peace be removed,"*
*   says the LORD, who has compassion on you.*

ISAIAH 54:10

Those who walk uprightly
*   enter into peace;*
*   they find rest as they lie in death.*

ISAIAH 57:2 TNIV

Jesus said, "Peace I leave with you; my peace I give you. I do not give to you as the world gives. Do not let your hearts be troubled and do not be afraid."

JOHN 14:27

Jesus said, "I have told you these things, so that in me you may have peace. In this world you will have trouble. But take heart! I have overcome the world."

JOHN 16:33

Peace

Whatever is true, whatever is noble, whatever is right, whatever is pure, whatever is lovely, whatever is admirable—if anything is excellent or praiseworthy—think about such things. Whatever you have learned or received or heard from me, or seen in me—put it into practice. And the God of peace will be with you.

PHILIPPIANS 4:8–9

All your children will be taught by the LORD,
and great will be their peace.

ISAIAH 54:13 TNIV

Do not be anxious about anything, but in everything, by prayer and petition, with thanksgiving, present your requests to God. And the peace of God, which transcends all understanding, will guard your hearts and your minds in Christ Jesus.

PHILIPPIANS 4:6–7

[Christ] himself is our peace.

EPHESIANS 2:14

Peacemakers who sow in peace raise a harvest of righteousness.

JAMES 3:18

Praise and Worship

I will praise you, O Lord my God, with all my heart;
*   I will glorify your name forever.*
For great is your love toward me,
*   you have delivered me from the depths of*
*   the grave.*

PSALM 86:12–13

The heavens praise your wonders, O LORD,
*   your faithfulness too, in the assembly of the*
*   holy ones.*

PSALM 89:5

I urge you ... in view of God's mercy, to offer your
bodies as living sacrifices, holy and pleasing to
God—this is your spiritual act of worship.

ROMANS 12:1

Let everything that has breath praise the LORD.

PSALM 150:6

Come, let us bow down in worship,
*   let us kneel before the LORD our Maker.*

PSALM 95:6

Praise and Worship

The trumpeters and singers joined in unison, as with one voice, to give praise and thanks to the LORD. Accompanied by trumpets, cymbals and other instruments, they raised their voices in praise to the LORD and sang:

"He is good;
his love endures forever."

Then the temple of the LORD was filled with a cloud, and the priests could not perform their service because of the cloud, for the glory of the LORD filled the temple of God.

2 CHRONICLES 5:13–14

Whenever the living creatures give glory, honor and thanks to him who sits on the throne and who lives for ever and ever, the twenty-four elders fall down before him who sits on the throne, and worship him who lives for ever and ever. They lay their crowns before the throne and say:

"You are worthy, our Lord and God,
to receive glory and honor and power,
for you created all things,
and by your will they were created
and have their being."

REVELATION 4:9–11

Praise and Worship

Enter his gates with thanksgiving
and his courts with praise;
give thanks to him and praise his name.

PSALM 100:4

Praise be to the God and Father of our Lord Jesus
Christ, who has blessed us in the heavenly realms
with every spiritual blessing in Christ.

EPHESIANS 1:3

Through Jesus, therefore, let us continually offer
to God a sacrifice of praise—the fruit of lips that
confess his name.

HEBREWS 13:15

Is any one of you in trouble? He should pray. Is
anyone happy? Let him sing songs of praise.

JAMES 5:13

If you suffer as a Christian, do not be ashamed, but
praise God that you bear that name.

1 PETER 4:16

Praise and Worship

O LORD, you are my God;
I will exalt you and praise your name,
for in perfect faithfulness
    you have done marvelous things,
    things planned long ago.

ISAIAH 25:1

Ascribe to the LORD the glory due his name;
    worship the LORD in the splendor of his holiness.

PSALM 29:2

Worship the LORD with gladness;
    come before him with joyful songs.

PSALM 100:2

From the lips of children and infants
    you have ordained praise
because of your enemies,
    to silence the foe and the avenger.

PSALM 8:2

Praise and Worship

Exalt the LORD our God
  and worship at his footstool;
  he is holy.

PSALM 99:5

I will praise the LORD, who counsels me;
  even at night my heart instructs me.

PSALM 16:7

I call to the LORD, who is worthy of praise,
  and I am saved from my enemies.

PSALM 18:3

Sing joyfully to the LORD, you righteous;
  it is fitting for the upright to praise him.
Praise the LORD with the harp;
  make music to him on the ten-stringed lyre.
Sing to him a new song;
  play skillfully, and shout for joy.

PSALM 33:1–3

Praise and Worship

I will praise you, O Lord, among the nations;
*   I will sing of you among the peoples.*
For great is your love, reaching to the heavens;
*   your faithfulness reaches to the skies.*
Be exalted, O God, above the heavens;
*   let your glory be over all the earth.*

PSALM 57:9–11

I will praise you forever for what you have done;
*   in your name I will hope, for your name is good.*
*   I will praise you in the presence of your saints.*

PSALM 52:9

The LORD lives! Praise be to my Rock!
*   Exalted be God my Savior!*

PSALM 18:46

I will extol the LORD at all times;
*   his praise will always be on my lips.*

PSALM 34:1

prayer

In my distress I called to the LORD,
  and he answered me.
From the depths of the grave I called for help,
  and you listened to my cry.

JONAH 2:2

They will not toil in vain
  or bear children doomed to misfortune;
for they will be a people blessed by the LORD,
  they and their descendants with them.
Before they call I will answer;
  while they are still speaking I will hear.

ISAIAH 65:23–24

Jesus said, "If you believe, you will receive whatever you ask for in prayer."

MATTHEW 21:22

Jesus said, "In that day you will no longer ask me anything. I tell you the truth, my Father will give you whatever you ask in my name. Until now you have not asked for anything in my name. Ask and you will receive, and your joy will be complete."

JOHN 16:23–24

Prayer

[The LORD] will respond to the prayer of the destitute;
    he will not despise their plea.
Let this be written for a future generation,
    that a people not yet created may praise
the LORD.

PSALM 102:17–18

Jesus said, "Ask and it will be given to you; seek
and you will find; knock and the door will be
opened to you. For everyone who asks receives;
those who seek find; and to those who knock, the
door will be opened."

MATTHEW 7:7–8 TNIV

This is the confidence we have in approaching God:
that if we ask anything according to his will, he
hears us. And if we know that he hears us — whatever we ask — we know that we have what we asked
of him.

1 JOHN 5:14–15

The LORD has heard my weeping.
The LORD has heard my cry for mercy;
    the LORD accepts my prayer.

PSALM 6:8–9

Prayer

Jesus said, "When you pray, go into your room, close the door and pray to your Father, who is unseen. Then your Father, who sees what is done in secret, will reward you."

MATTHEW 6:6

"If my people ... will ... pray and ... turn from their wicked ways, then will I hear from heaven and will forgive their sin and will heal their land," declares the LORD.

2 CHRONICLES 7:14

Jesus said, "When you stand praying, if you hold anything against anyone, forgive them, so that your Father in heaven may forgive you your sins."

MARK 11:25 TNIV

Pray in the Spirit on all occasions with all kinds of prayers and requests. With this in mind, be alert and always keep on praying for all the saints.

EPHESIANS 6:18

"You will call upon me and come and pray to me, and I will listen to you," says the LORD. "You will seek me and find me when you seek me with all your heart."

JEREMIAH 29:12–13

Prayer

[God] does not ignore the cry of the afflicted.

PSALM 9:12

Now I know that the LORD saves his anointed;
he answers him from his holy heaven
with the saving power of his right hand.

PSALM 20:6

Cast your cares on the LORD
and he will sustain you;
he will never let the righteous fall.

PSALM 55:22

I call on you, O God, for you will answer me;
give ear to me and hear my prayer.

PSALM 17:6

To the LORD I cry aloud,
and he answers me from his holy hill.

PSALM 3:4

Prayer

I call to God,
*and the L*ORD *saves me.*
Evening, morning and noon
I cry out in distress,
and he hears my voice.

PSALM 55:16–17

Do not be anxious about anything, but in everything, by prayer and petition, with thanksgiving, present your requests to God. And the peace of God, which transcends all understanding, will guard your hearts and your minds in Christ Jesus.

PHILIPPIANS 4:6–7

If I had cherished sin in my heart,
the Lord would not have listened;
but God has surely listened
and heard my voice in prayer.
Praise be to God,
who has not rejected my prayer
or withheld his love from me!

PSALM 66:18–20

Prayer

Jesus said, "Again, I tell you that if two of you on earth agree about anything you ask for, it will be done for you by my Father in heaven."

MATTHEW 18:19

Jesus said, "I will do whatever you ask in my name, so that the Son may bring glory to the Father. You may ask me for anything in my name, and I will do it."

JOHN 14:13–14

The LORD is near to all who call on him,
*   to all who call on him in truth.*
He fulfills the desires of those who fear him;
*   he hears their cry and saves them.*

PSALM 145:18–19

"Call upon me in the day of trouble;
*   I will deliver you, and you will honor me,"*
*   declares the LORD.*

PSALM 50:15

Jesus said, "Whatever you ask for in prayer, believe that you have received it, and it will be yours."

MARK 11:24

Pride and Humility

To fear the LORD is to hate evil;
I, [wisdom], hate pride and arrogance,
evil behavior and perverse speech.

PROVERBS 8:13

When pride comes, then comes disgrace,
but with humility comes wisdom.

PROVERBS 11:2

Pride only breeds quarrels,
but wisdom is found in those who take advice.

PROVERBS 13:10

Better to be lowly in spirit and among the oppressed
than to share plunder with the proud.

PROVERBS 16:19

The end of a matter is better than its beginning,
and patience is better than pride.

ECCLESIASTES 7:8

Pride and Humility

Pride brings a person low,
but the lowly in spirit gain honor.

PROVERBS 29:23 TNIV

[The LORD] guides the humble in what is right
and teaches them his way.

PSALM 25:9

The LORD sustains the humble
but casts the wicked to the ground.

PSALM 147:6

Remind the people to be subject to rulers and
authorities, to be obedient, to be ready to do whatever is good, to slander no one, to be peaceable and
considerate, and to show true humility toward all.

TITUS 3:1–2

As God's chosen people, holy and dearly loved,
clothe yourselves with compassion, kindness, humility, gentleness and patience.

COLOSSIANS 3:12

Pride and Humility

You, [LORD], save the humble
  but bring low those whose eyes are haughty.

PSALM 18:27

[The LORD] mocks proud mockers
  but gives grace to the humble.

PROVERBS 3:34

The LORD declares,
"This is the one I esteem:
  he who is humble and contrite in spirit,
  and trembles at my word."

ISAIAH 66:2

The Lord said, "If my people, who are called by my name, will humble themselves and pray and seek my face and turn from their wicked ways, then will I hear from heaven and will forgive their sin and will heal their land."

2 CHRONICLES 7:14

Pride and Humility

Do not think of yourself more highly than you ought, but rather think of yourself with sober judgment, in accordance with the measure of faith God has given you.

ROMANS 12:3

You, [O LORD], save the humble,
    but your eyes are on the haughty to bring them low.

2 SAMUEL 22:28

Jesus said, "The greatest among you will be your servant. For those who exalt themselves will be humbled, and those who humble themselves will be exalted."

MATTHEW 23:11–12 TNIV

Clothe yourselves with humility toward one another, because,

"God opposes the proud
    but gives grace to the humble."

Humble yourselves, therefore, under God's mighty hand, that he may lift you up in due time.

1 PETER 5:5–6

Pride and Humility

Humility and the fear of the LORD
bring wealth and honor and life.

PROVERBS 22:4

Before a downfall the heart is haughty,
but humility comes before honor.

PROVERBS 18:12 TNIV

Be completely humble and gentle; be patient, bearing with one another in love.

EPHESIANS 4:2

Be like-minded, be sympathetic, love one another, be compassionate and humble.

1 PETER 3:8 TNIV

The fear of the LORD teaches a man wisdom,
and humility comes before honor.

PROVERBS 15:33

Do nothing out of selfish ambition or vain conceit, but in humility consider others better than yourselves.

PHILIPPIANS 2:3

Pride and Humility

The LORD takes delight in his people;
he crowns the humble with salvation.

PSALM 149:4

Humble yourselves before the Lord, and he will lift you up.

JAMES 4:10

Who is wise and understanding among you? Let them show it by their good life, by deeds done in the humility that comes from wisdom.

JAMES 3:13 TNIV

My heart is not proud, O LORD,
my eyes are not haughty;
I do not concern myself with great matters
or things too wonderful for me.
But I have stilled and quieted my soul;
like a weaned child with its mother,
like a weaned child is my soul within me.

PSALM 131:1–2

Redemption

If you confess with your mouth, "Jesus is Lord," and believe in your heart that God raised him from the dead, you will be saved. For it is with your heart that you believe and are justified, and it is with your mouth that you confess and are saved.

ROMANS 10:9–10

[The LORD] provided redemption for his people;
he ordained his covenant forever—
holy and awesome is his name.

PSALM 111:9

Put your hope in the LORD,
for with the LORD is unfailing love
and with him is full redemption.

PSALM 130:7

Christ redeemed us from the curse of the law by becoming a curse for us, for it is written: "Cursed is everyone who is hung on a tree." He redeemed us in order that the blessing given to Abraham might come to the Gentiles through Christ Jesus, so that by faith we might receive the promise of the Spirit.

GALATIANS 3:13–14

Redemption

It is because of [God] that you are in Christ Jesus,
who has become for us wisdom from God—that is,
our righteousness, holiness and redemption.

1 CORINTHIANS 1:30

In him we have redemption through his blood, the
forgiveness of sins, in accordance with the riches of
God's grace.

EPHESIANS 1:7

He has rescued us from the dominion of darkness
and brought us into the kingdom of the Son he loves,
in whom we have redemption, the forgiveness
of sins.

COLOSSIANS 1:13–14

[Christ] did not enter by means of the blood of goats
and calves; but he entered the Most Holy Place once
for all by his own blood, having obtained
eternal redemption.

HEBREWS 9:12

My lips will shout for joy
    when I sing praise to you—
    I, whom you have redeemed.

PSALM 71:23

Redemption

Let the redeemed of the LORD say this —
those he redeemed from the hand of the foe.

PSALM 107:2

This is what the LORD says,

"Fear not, for I have redeemed you;
I have summoned you by name; you are mine.

ISAIAH 43:1

The LORD says,
"I have swept away your offenses like a cloud,
your sins like the morning mist.
Return to me,
for I have redeemed you."

ISAIAH 44:22

You know that it was not with perishable things
such as silver or gold that you were redeemed from
the empty way of life handed down to you from your
forefathers, but with the precious blood of Christ, a
lamb without blemish or defect.

1 PETER 1:18–19

Redemption

God will redeem my life from the grave;
* he will surely take me to himself.*

PSALM 49:15

Redeem me from the oppression of men,
* that I may obey your precepts.*

PSALM 119:134

Defend my cause and redeem me;
* preserve my life according to your promise.*

PSALM 119:154

We ... who have the firstfruits of the Spirit, groan inwardly as we wait eagerly for our adoption, the redemption of our bodies.

ROMANS 8:23 TNIV

We wait for the blessed hope—the glorious appearing of our great God and Savior, Jesus Christ, who gave himself for us to redeem us from all wickedness and to purify for himself a people that are his very own, eager to do what is good.

TITUS 2:13–14

Redemption

When the set time had fully come, God sent his Son, born of a woman, born under the law, to redeem those under the law, that we might receive adoption to sonship. Because you are his sons, God sent the Spirit of his Son into our hearts, the Spirit who calls out, *"Abba*, Father." So you are no longer slaves, but God's children; and since you are his children, he has made you also heirs.

GALATIANS 4:4–7 TNIV

All have sinned and fall short of the glory of God, and are justified freely by his grace through the redemption that came by Christ Jesus.

ROMANS 3:23–24

The Lord says,
"I will ransom them from the power
of the grave;
I will redeem them from death.
Where, O death, are your plagues?
Where, O grave, is your destruction?"

HOSEA 13:14

Redemption

There is one God and one mediator between God and human beings, Christ Jesus, himself human, who gave himself as a ransom for all people.

1 TIMOTHY 2:5–6 TNIV

Job said, "I know that my Redeemer lives."

JOB 19:25

"This is what the LORD says—
    Israel's King and Redeemer, the LORD Almighty:
I am the first and I am the last;
    apart from me there is no God."

ISAIAH 44:6

The LORD says,
"Your Maker is your husband—
    the LORD Almighty is his name—
the Holy One of Israel is your Redeemer;
    he is called the God of all the earth."

ISAIAH 54:5

Relationships

Accept one another, then, just as Christ accepted you, in order to bring praise to God.

ROMANS 15:7

Carry each other's burdens, and in this way you will fulfill the law of Christ.

GALATIANS 6:2

Confess your sins to each other and pray for each other so that you may be healed. The prayer of a righteous person is powerful and effective.

JAMES 5:16 TNIV

Let no debt remain outstanding, except the continuing debt to love one another, for whoever loves others has fulfilled the law. The commandments ... are summed up in this one command: "Love your neighbor as yourself." Love does no harm to its neighbor. Therefore love is the fulfillment of the law.

ROMANS 13:8–10 TNIV

Be devoted to one another in brotherly love. Honor one another above yourselves.

ROMANS 12:10

Relationships

Walk with the wise and become wise.

PROVERBS 13:20 TNIV

I appeal to you ... in the name of our Lord Jesus
Christ, that all of you agree with one another so that
there may be no divisions among you and that you
may be perfectly united in mind and thought.

1 CORINTHIANS 1:10

Jesus said, "A new command I give you: Love one
another. As I have loved you, so you must love
one another."

JOHN 13:34

Live in harmony with one another. Do not be proud,
but be willing to associate with people of low posi-
tion. Do not be conceited. Do not repay anyone evil
for evil. Be careful to do what is right in the eyes of
everybody. If it is possible, as far as it depends on
you, live at peace with everyone.

ROMANS 12:16–18

Relationships

Let us stop passing judgment on one another. Instead, make up your mind not to put any stumbling block or obstacle in the way of a brother or sister.

ROMANS 14:13 TNIV

Everyone should be quick to listen, slow to speak and slow to become angry.

JAMES 1:19

You, my brothers and sisters, were called to be free. But do not use your freedom to indulge the sinful nature; rather, serve one another humbly in love. For the entire law is fulfilled in keeping this one command: "Love your neighbor as yourself." If you keep on biting and devouring each other, watch out or you will be destroyed by each other.

GALATIANS 5:13–15 TNIV

Be completely humble and gentle; be patient, bearing with one another in love. Make every effort to keep the unity of the Spirit through the bond of peace.

EPHESIANS 4:2–3

Submit to one another out of reverence for Christ.

EPHESIANS 5:21

Relationships

Bear with each other and forgive whatever grievances you may have against one another. Forgive as the Lord forgave you. And over all these virtues put on love, which binds them all together in perfect unity. Let the peace of Christ rule in your hearts, since as members of one body you were called to peace. And be thankful. Let the word of Christ dwell in you richly as you teach and admonish one another with all wisdom, and as you sing psalms, hymns and spiritual songs with gratitude in your hearts to God.

COLOSSIANS 3:13–16

Encourage one another and build each other up, just as in fact you are doing.

1 THESSALONIANS 5:11

Let us consider how we may spur one another on toward love and good deeds. Let us not give up meeting together, as some are in the habit of doing, but let us encourage one another—and all the more as you see the Day approaching.

HEBREWS 10:24–25

Relationships

Now that you have purified yourselves by obeying the truth so that you have sincere love for each other, love one another deeply, from the heart.

1 PETER 1:22 TNIV

Be like-minded, be sympathetic, love one another, be compassionate and humble. Do not repay evil with evil or insult with insult. On the contrary, repay evil with blessing, because to this you were called so that you may inherit a blessing.

1 PETER 3:8–9 TNIV

Offer hospitality to one another without grumbling. Each one should use whatever gift he has received to serve others.

1 PETER 4:9–10

You who are younger, submit yourselves to your elders. All of you, clothe yourselves with humility toward one another, because,

"God opposes the proud
but shows favor to the humble and oppressed."

1 PETER 5:5 TNIV

Relationships

Dear friends, since God so loved us, we also ought to love one another. No one has ever seen God; but if we love one another, God lives in us and his love is made complete in us.

1 JOHN 4:11–12

Jesus said, "My command is this: Love each other as I have loved you. Greater love has no one than this: to lay down one's life for one's friends."

JOHN 15:12–13 TNIV

God has combined the members of the body and has given greater honor to the parts that lacked it, so that there should be no division in the body, but that its parts should have equal concern for each other. If one part suffers, every part suffers with it; if one part is honored, every part rejoices with it.

1 CORINTHIANS 12:24–26

Be kind and compassionate to one another, forgiving each other, just as in Christ God forgave you. Be imitators of God, therefore, as dearly loved children and live a life of love, just as Christ loved us and gave himself up for us.

EPHESIANS 4:32—5:2

Restoration

Jesus said, "Come to me, all you who are weary
and burdened, and I will give you rest. Take my
yoke upon you and learn from me, for I am gentle
and humble in heart, and you will find rest for your
souls. For my yoke is easy and my burden is light."

MATTHEW 11:28–30

My soul finds rest in God alone;
my salvation comes from him.
He alone is my rock and my salvation;
he is my fortress, I will never be shaken.

PSALM 62:1–2

There remains ... a Sabbath-rest for the people of
God; for anyone who enters God's rest also rests
from his own work, just as God did from his. Let us,
therefore, make every effort to enter that rest.

HEBREWS 4:9–11

My people will live in peaceful dwelling places,
in secure homes,
in undisturbed places of rest.

ISAIAH 32:18

Restoration

He who dwells in the shelter of the Most High
   will rest in the shadow of the Almighty.

PSALM 91:1

The LORD is my shepherd, I shall not be in want.
   He makes me lie down in green pastures,
he leads me beside quiet waters,
   he restores my soul.
He guides me in paths of righteousness
   for his name's sake.

PSALM 23:1–3

Be at rest once more, O my soul,
   for the LORD has been good to you.

PSALM 116:7

Repent, then, and turn to God, so that your sins may
be wiped out, that times of refreshing may come
from the Lord.

ACTS 3:19

Restoration

Though you have made me see troubles, many
  and bitter,
    you will restore my life again;
from the depths of the earth
    you will again bring me up.
You will increase my honor
    and comfort me once again.

PSALM 71:20–21

"I will restore you to health
    and heal your wounds,"
        declares the LORD.

JEREMIAH 30:17

When you and your children return to the LORD
your God and obey him with all your heart and with
all your soul according to everything I command
you today, then the LORD your God will restore your
fortunes and have compassion on you.

DEUTERONOMY 30:2–3

The LORD says, "I will search for the lost and bring
back the strays. I will bind up the injured and
strengthen the weak."

EZEKIEL 34:16

Restoration

Restore us, O God;
make your face shine upon us,
that we may be saved.

PSALM 80:3

The God of all grace, who called you to his eternal glory in Christ, after you have suffered a little while, will himself restore you and make you strong, firm and steadfast.

1 PETER 5:10

The LORD says,
"I will repay you for the years
the locusts have eaten—
the great locust and the young locust,
the other locusts and the locust swarm—
my great army that I sent among you.
You will have plenty to eat, until you are full,
and you will praise the name of the LORD
your God,
who has worked wonders for you;
never again will my people be shamed."

JOEL 2:25–26

Restoration

This is what the LORD Almighty says: "I will refresh
the weary and satisfy the faint."

JEREMIAH 31:25

Do you not know?
  Have you not heard?
The LORD is the everlasting God,
  the Creator of the ends of the earth.
He will not grow tired or weary,
  and his understanding no one can fathom.
He gives strength to the weary
  and increases the power of the weak.
Even youths grow tired and weary,
  and young men stumble and fall;
but those who hope in the LORD
  will renew their strength.
They will soar on wings like eagles;
  they will run and not grow weary,
  they will walk and not be faint.

ISAIAH 40:28–31

Restoration

Strengthen the feeble hands,
*   steady the knees that give way;*
say to those with fearful hearts,
*   "Be strong, do not fear;*
your God will come,
*   he will come with vengeance;*
with divine retribution
*   he will come to save you."*

ISAIAH 35:3–4

The LORD will guide you always;
*   he will satisfy your needs in a sun-scorched land*
*   and will strengthen your frame.*
You will be like a well-watered garden,
*   like a spring whose waters never fail.*

ISAIAH 58:11

I pray that out of his glorious riches he may
strengthen you with power through his Spirit in your
inner being.

EPHESIANS 3:16

Righteousness

*Whoever pursues righteousness and love
    finds life, prosperity and honor.*

PROVERBS 21:21 TNIV

*In the way of righteousness there is life;
    along that path is immortality.*

PROVERBS 12:28

*[God] does not take his eyes off the righteous;
    he enthrones them with kings
    and exalts them forever.*

JOB 36:7

*The path of the righteous is like the first gleam
        of dawn,
    shining ever brighter till the full light of day.*

PROVERBS 4:18

*The fruit of the righteous is a tree of life,
    and those who win souls are wise.*

PROVERBS 11:30 TNIV

Righteousness

Jesus said,
*"Blessed are those who hunger and thirst
    for righteousness,
    for they will be filled."*

MATTHEW 5:6

God made him who had no sin to be sin for us, so that in him we might become the righteousness of God.

2 CORINTHIANS 5:21

Do not let anyone lead you astray. The one who does what is right is righteous, just as he is righteous.

1 JOHN 3:7 TNIV

*The righteous will inherit the land
    and dwell in it forever.
The mouths of the righteous utter wisdom,
    and their tongues speak what is just.
The law of their God is in their hearts;
    their feet do not slip.*

PSALM 37:29–31 TNIV

Righteousness

Sow for yourselves righteousness,
*   reap the fruit of unfailing love,*
and break up your unplowed ground;
*   for it is time to seek the LORD,*
until he comes
*   and showers righteousness on you.*

HOSEA 10:12

Surely the righteous will never be shaken;
*   they will be remembered forever.*
They will have no fear of bad news;
*   their hearts are steadfast, trusting in the LORD.*

PSALM 112:6–7 TNIV

No harm overtakes the righteous,
*   but the wicked have their fill of trouble.*

PROVERBS 12:21 TNIV

The righteous are as bold as a lion.

PROVERBS 28:1

Righteousness

The eyes of the Lord are on the righteous
*   and his ears are attentive to their prayer.*

1 PETER 3:12

The prayer of a righteous person is powerful
and effective.

JAMES 5:16 TNIV

The fruit of righteousness will be peace;
*   the effect of righteousness will be quietness and*
confidence forever.

ISAIAH 32:17

For you who revere my name, the sun of righteousness will rise with healing in its wings. And you will
go out and leap like calves released from the stall.

MALACHI 4:2

Jesus said,
"Blessed are those who are persecuted because
of righteousness,
*   for theirs is the kingdom of heaven."*

MATTHEW 5:10

Righteousness

All Scripture is God-breathed and is useful for teaching, rebuking, correcting and training in righteousness.

2 TIMOTHY 3:16

In the gospel a righteousness from God is revealed, a righteousness that is by faith from first to last, just as it is written: "The righteous will live by faith."

ROMANS 1:17

Righteousness from God comes through faith in Jesus Christ to all who believe.

ROMANS 3:22

I consider everything a loss compared to the surpassing greatness of knowing Christ Jesus my Lord, for whose sake I have lost all things. I consider them rubbish, that I may gain Christ and be found in him, not having a righteousness of my own that comes from the law, but that which is through faith in Christ — the righteousness that comes from God and is by faith.

PHILIPPIANS 3:8–9

Peacemakers who sow in peace raise a harvest of righteousness.

JAMES 3:18

Righteousness

God made him who had no sin to be sin for us, so that in him we might become the righteousness of God.

2 CORINTHIANS 5:21

No discipline seems pleasant at the time, but painful. Later on, however, it produces a harvest of righteousness and peace for those who have been trained by it.

HEBREWS 12:11

He himself bore our sins in his body on the tree, so that we might die to sins and live for righteousness.

1 PETER 2:24

In keeping with his promise we are looking forward to a new heaven and a new earth, the home of righteousness.

2 PETER 3:13

Where sin increased, grace increased all the more, so that, just as sin reigned in death, so also grace might reign through righteousness to bring eternal life through Jesus Christ our Lord.

ROMANS 5:20–21

Sacrifice

O LORD, open my lips,
and my mouth will declare your praise.
The sacrifices of God are a broken spirit;
a broken and contrite heart,
O God, you will not despise.

PSALM 51:15, 17

I urge you, ... in view of God's mercy, to offer your bodies as living sacrifices, holy and pleasing to God—this is your spiritual act of worship.

ROMANS 12:1

I will sacrifice a freewill offering to you;
I will praise your name, O LORD,
for it is good.
For he has delivered me from all my troubles,
and my eyes have looked in triumph on my foes.

PSALM 54:6–7

To obey is better than sacrifice,
and to heed is better than the fat of rams.

1 SAMUEL 15:22

Sacrifice

To do what is right and just
*   is more acceptable to the LORD than sacrifice.*
                                        PROVERBS 21:3

As you come to him, the living Stone — rejected by
men but chosen by God and precious to him — you
also, like living stones, are being built into a spiritual house to be a holy priesthood, offering spiritual
sacrifices acceptable to God through Jesus Christ.
                                        1 PETER 2:4–5

Through Jesus ... let us continually offer to God a
sacrifice of praise — the fruit of lips that confess
his name. And do not forget to do good and to share
with others, for with such sacrifices God is pleased.
                                        HEBREWS 13:15–16

The LORD says,
"Sacrifice thank offerings to God,
*   fulfill your vows to the Most High,*
and call upon me in the day of trouble;
*   I will deliver you, and you will honor me."*
                                        PSALM 50:14–15

Sacrifice

In the day of trouble
    he will keep me safe in his dwelling;
he will hide me in the shelter of his tabernacle
    and set me high upon a rock.
Then my head will be exalted
    above the enemies who surround me;
at his tabernacle will I sacrifice with shouts of joy;
    I will sing and make music to the LORD.

PSALM 27:5–6

Let them give thanks to the LORD for his
        unfailing love
and his wonderful deeds for men.
Let them sacrifice thank offerings
    and tell of his works with songs of joy.

PSALM 107:21–22

All have sinned and fall short of the glory of God, and are justified freely by his grace through the redemption that came by Christ Jesus. God presented him as a sacrifice of atonement, through faith in his blood. He did this to demonstrate his justice.

ROMANS 3:23–25

Sacrifice

Be imitators of God, therefore, as dearly loved children and live a life of love, just as Christ loved us and gave himself up for us as a fragrant offering and sacrifice to God.

EPHESIANS 5:1–2

The LORD detests the sacrifice of the wicked,
but the prayer of the upright pleases him.

PROVERBS 15:8

Christ did not enter a man-made sanctuary that was only a copy of the true one; he entered heaven itself, now to appear for us in God's presence. Nor did he enter heaven to offer himself again and again, the way the high priest enters the Most Holy Place every year with blood that is not his own. Then Christ would have had to suffer many times since the creation of the world. But now he has appeared once for all at the end of the ages to do away with sin by the sacrifice of himself.

HEBREWS 9:24–26

Jesus Christ, the Righteous One, is the atoning sacrifice for our sins, and not only for ours but also for the sins of the whole world.

1 JOHN 2:1–2

Sacrifice

This is love: not that we loved God, but that he loved us and sent his Son as an atoning sacrifice for our sins.

1 JOHN 4:10

God demonstrates his own love for us in this: While we were still sinners, Christ died for us. Since we have now been justified by his blood, how much more shall we be saved from God's wrath through him!

ROMANS 5:8–9

We have been made holy through the sacrifice of the body of Jesus Christ once for all. Day after day every priest stands and performs his religious duties; again and again he offers the same sacrifices, which can never take away sins. But when this priest had offered for all time one sacrifice for sins, he sat down at the right hand of God. Since that time he waits for his enemies to be made his footstool, because by one sacrifice he has made perfect forever those who are being made holy.

HEBREWS 10:10–14

Sacrifice

O LORD, I call to you; come quickly to me.
Hear my voice when I call to you.
May my prayer be set before you like incense;
may the lifting up of my hands be like the
evening sacrifice.

PSALM 141:1–2

Jesus took bread, gave thanks and broke it, and
gave it to his disciples, saying, "Take and eat; this
is my body." Then he took the cup, gave thanks and
offered it to them, saying, "Drink from it, all of you.
This is my blood of the covenant, which is poured
out for many for the forgiveness of sins."

MATTHEW 26:26–28

God was pleased to have all his fullness dwell in
him, and through him to reconcile to himself all
things, whether things on earth or things in heaven,
by making peace through his blood, shed on the
cross.... He has reconciled you by Christ's physical
body through death to present you holy in his sight,
without blemish and free from accusation.

COLOSSIANS 1:19–20, 22

Self-Image

"This is what the LORD says—
    your Redeemer, who formed you in the womb:
I am the LORD,
who has made all things,
who alone stretched out the heavens,
who spread out the earth by myself."

ISAIAH 44:24

[God] chose us in him before the creation of the world to be holy and blameless in his sight. In love he predestined us to be adopted as his sons through Jesus Christ, in accordance with his pleasure and will.

EPHESIANS 1:4–5

Don't you know that you yourselves are God's temple and that God's Spirit lives in you?

1 CORINTHIANS 3:16

Know that the LORD is God.
    It is he who made us, and we are his;
    we are his people, the sheep of his pasture.

PSALM 100:3

Self-Image

Jesus said, "Are not two sparrows sold for a penny? Yet not one of them will fall to the ground apart from the will of your Father. And even the very hairs of your head are all numbered. So don't be afraid; you are worth more than many sparrows."

MATTHEW 10:29–31

For you created my inmost being;
   you knit me together in my mother's womb.
I praise you because I am fearfully and
      wonderfully made;
   your works are wonderful,
   I know that full well.

PSALM 139:13–14

Do you not know that your body is a temple of the Holy Spirit, who is in you, whom you have received from God? You are not your own; you were bought at a price. Therefore honor God with your body.

1 CORINTHIANS 6:19–20

You have put on the new self, which is being re-newed in knowledge in the image of its Creator.

COLOSSIANS 3:10

Self-Image

*What are mere mortals that you are mindful
    of them,
    human beings that you care for them?
You have made them a little lower than the
        heavenly beings
    and crowned them with glory and honor.
You made them rulers over the works of your hands;
    you put everything under their feet.*

PSALM 8:4–6 TNIV

God created human beings in his own image, in the
image of God he created them; male and female he
created them.

GENESIS 1:27 TNIV

The LORD declares,
*"Can a mother forget the baby at her breast
    and have no compassion on the child she
        has borne?
Though she may forget,
    I will not forget you!
See, I have engraved you on the palms of my hands;
    your walls are ever before me."*

ISAIAH 49:15–16

Self-Image

The LORD says,
*"You are precious and honored in my sight,
    and ... I love you."*

ISAIAH 43:4

The LORD said,
*"Before I formed you in the womb I knew you,
    before you were born I set you apart;
    I appointed you as a prophet to the nations."*

JEREMIAH 1:5

You are no longer slaves, but God's children; and
since you are his children, he has made you
also heirs.

GALATIANS 4:7 TNIV

"From one man he made all the nations, that they
should inhabit the whole earth; and he marked out
their appointed times in history and the boundaries
of their lands.... 'For in him we live and move and
have our being.' As some of your own poets have
said, 'We are his offspring.'"

ACTS 17:26, 28 TNIV

Self-Image

Do not think of yourself more highly than you ought, but rather think of yourself with sober judgment, in accordance with the measure of faith God has given you.

ROMANS 12:3

We are God's workmanship, created in Christ Jesus to do good works, which God prepared in advance for us to do.

EPHESIANS 2:10

This is what the LORD says—
    he who created you, O Jacob,
    he who formed you, O Israel:
"Fear not, for I have redeemed you;
    I have summoned you by name; you are mine."

ISAIAH 43:1

Since we have confidence to enter the Most Holy Place by the blood of Jesus ... let us draw near to God with a sincere heart in full assurance of faith, having our hearts sprinkled to cleanse us from a guilty conscience and having our bodies washed with pure water.

HEBREWS 10:19, 22

Self-Image

I pray that out of his glorious riches he may
strengthen you with power through his Spirit in your
inner being, so that Christ may dwell in your hearts
through faith. And I pray that you, being rooted and
established in love, may have power, together with
all the saints, to grasp how wide and long and high
and deep is the love of Christ, and to know this love
that surpasses knowledge—that you may be filled
to the measure of all the fullness of God.

EPHESIANS 3:16–19

The LORD appeared to us in the past, saying:

"I have loved you with an everlasting love;
    I have drawn you with loving-kindness."

JEREMIAH 31:3

Show the wonder of your great love,
    you who save by your right hand
    those who take refuge in you from their foes.
Keep me as the apple of your eye;
    hide me in the shadow of your wings.

PSALM 17:7–8

Service

Do you see those who are skilled in their work?
They will serve before kings;
they will not serve before officials of low rank.

PROVERBS 22:29 TNIV

This is what the LORD says:

"If you repent, I will restore you
that you may serve me."

JEREMIAH 15:19

What does the LORD your God ask of you but to fear
the LORD your God, to walk in all his ways, to love
him, to serve the LORD your God with all your heart
and with all your soul, and to observe the LORD'S
commands and decrees.

DEUTERONOMY 10:12–13

No one can serve two masters. Either you will hate
the one and love the other, or you will be devoted
to the one and despise the other. You cannot serve
both God and Money.

MATTHEW 6:24 TNIV

Service

There are different kinds of gifts, but the same
Spirit. There are different kinds of service, but the
same Lord.

1 CORINTHIANS 12:4–5

Jesus said, "Whoever wants to become great among
you must be your servant, and whoever wants to be
first must be your slave — just as the Son of Man did
not come to be served, but to serve, and to give his
life as a ransom for many."

MATTHEW 20:26–28

Now, by dying to what once bound us, we have been
released from the law so that we serve in the new
way of the Spirit, and not in the old way of the written code.

ROMANS 7:6

We have different gifts, according to the grace given
to each of us. If your gift is ... serving, then serve.

ROMANS 12:6–7 TNIV

You, my brothers and sisters, were called to be free.
But do not use your freedom to indulge the sinful
nature; rather, serve one another humbly in love.

GALATIANS 5:13 TNIV

Service

Serve wholeheartedly, as if you were serving the Lord, not people, because you know that the Lord will reward each one of you for whatever good you do, whether you are slave or free.

EPHESIANS 6:7–8 TNIV

Those who have believing masters should not show them disrespect just because they are fellow believers. Instead, they should serve them even better because their masters are dear to them as fellow believers and are devoted to the welfare of their slaves.

1 TIMOTHY 6:2 TNIV

It was he who gave some to be apostles, ... prophets, ... evangelists, ... pastors and teachers, to prepare God's people for works of service.

EPHESIANS 4:11–12

The blood of goats and bulls and the ashes of a heifer sprinkled on those who are ceremonially unclean sanctify them so that they are outwardly clean. How much more, then, will the blood of Christ, who through the eternal Spirit offered himself unblemished to God, cleanse our consciences from acts that lead to death, so that we may serve the living God!

HEBREWS 9:13–14

Service

Be shepherds of God's flock that is under your care,
serving as overseers — not because you must, but
because you are willing, as God wants you to be;
not greedy for money, but eager to serve; not lording
it over those entrusted to you, but being examples
to the flock. And when the Chief Shepherd appears,
you will receive the crown of glory that will never
fade away.

1 PETER 5:2–4

This service that you perform is not only supplying
the needs of the Lord's people but is also overflowing in many expressions of thanks to God. Because
of the service by which you have proved yourselves,
people will praise God for the obedience that ac-
companies your confession of the gospel of Christ,
and for your generosity in sharing with them and
with everyone else.

2 CORINTHIANS 9:12–13 TNIV

Are not all angels ministering spirits sent to serve
those who will inherit salvation?

HEBREWS 1:14

Service

I glory in Christ Jesus in my service to God.

ROMANS 15:17

I thank Christ Jesus our Lord, who has given me strength, that he considered me faithful, appointing me to his service.

1 TIMOTHY 1:12

Whatever you do, work at it with all your heart, as working for the Lord, not for men, since you know that you will receive an inheritance from the Lord as a reward. It is the Lord Christ you are serving.

COLOSSIANS 3:23–24

To him who loves us and has freed us from our sins by his blood, and has made us to be a kingdom and priests to serve his God and Father—to him be glory and power for ever and ever! Amen.

REVELATION 1:5–6

He had to be made like his brothers and sisters in every way, in order that he might become a merciful and faithful high priest in service to God.

HEBREWS 2:17 TNIV

Service

Jesus said, "The greatest among you will be your servant. For those who exalt themselves will be humbled, and those who humble themselves will be exalted."

MATTHEW 23:11–12 TNIV

Jesus said, "Whoever serves me must follow me; and where I am, my servant also will be. My Father will honor the one who serves me."

JOHN 12:26

Am I now trying to win the approval of men, or of God? Or am I trying to please men? If I were still trying to please men, I would not be a servant of Christ.

GALATIANS 1:10

I became a servant of this gospel by the gift of God's grace given me through the working of his power.

EPHESIANS 3:7

The LORD be exalted,
who delights in the well-being of his servant.

PSALM 35:27

Strength

Those who hope in the LORD
will renew their strength.
They will soar on wings like eagles;
they will run and not grow weary,
they will walk and not be faint.

ISAIAH 40:31

The LORD gives strength to his people.

PSALM 29:11

I can do everything through [Christ] who gives
me strength.

PHILIPPIANS 4:13

God is our refuge and strength,
an ever-present help in trouble.

PSALM 46:1

You do not lack any spiritual gift as you eagerly wait
for our Lord Jesus Christ to be revealed. He will
keep you strong to the end.

1 CORINTHIANS 1:7–8

Strength

Blessed are those whose strength is in you,
  who have set their hearts on pilgrimage.
As they pass through the Valley of Baca,
  they make it a place of springs;
  the autumn rains also cover it with pools.
They go from strength to strength,
  till each appears before God in Zion.

PSALM 84:5–7

It is God who arms me with strength
  and makes my way perfect.
He makes my feet like the feet of a deer;
  he enables me to stand on the heights.

2 SAMUEL 22:33–34

I will sing of your strength,
  in the morning I will sing of your love;
for you are my fortress,
  my refuge in times of trouble.

PSALM 59:16

Strength

May he strengthen your hearts so that you will be
blameless and holy in the presence of our God and
Father when our Lord Jesus comes with all his
holy ones.

1 THESSALONIANS 3:13

O my Strength, I watch for you;
*   you, O God, are my fortress, my loving God.*
God will go before me
*   and will let me gloat over those who slander me.*

PSALM 59:9–10

My flesh and my heart may fail,
*   but God is the strength of my heart*
*   and my portion forever.*

PSALM 73:26

Do not fear, for I am with you;
*   do not be dismayed, for I am your God.*
I will strengthen you and help you;
*   I will uphold you with my righteous right hand.*

ISAIAH 41:10

Strength

The LORD is my strength and my shield;
my heart trusts in him, and I am helped.

PSALM 28:7

The LORD is my strength and my song;
he has become my salvation.
He is my God, and I will praise him,
my father's God, and I will exalt him.

EXODUS 15:2

The LORD is the strength of his people,
a fortress of salvation for his anointed one.

PSALM 28:8

I love you, O LORD, my strength.

PSALM 18:1

Strength

O my Strength, I sing praise to you;
*   you, O God, are my fortress, my loving God.*

PSALM 59:17

You are awesome, O God, in your sanctuary;
*   the God of Israel gives power and strength to*
*   his people.*

PSALM 68:35

The LORD reigns, he is robed in majesty;
*   the LORD is robed in majesty*
*   and is armed with strength.*
The world is firmly established;
*   it cannot be moved.*

PSALM 93:1

Blessed are those who have learned to acclaim you,
*   who walk in the light of your presence, O LORD.*
They rejoice in your name all day long;
*   they exult in your righteousness.*
For you are their glory and strength.

PSALM 89:15–17

Strength

Sing for joy to God our strength;
  shout aloud to the God of Jacob!

PSALM 81:1

Look to the LORD and his strength;
  seek his face always.

PSALM 105:4

The LORD is my strength and my song;
  he has become my salvation.

PSALM 118:14

The wise prevail through great power,
  and those who have knowledge muster
    their strength.

PROVERBS 24:5 TNIV

A wife of noble character who can find?
  She is clothed with strength and dignity.

PROVERBS 31:10, 25

Success

Commit to the LORD whatever you do,
and your plans will succeed.

PROVERBS 16:3

Plans fail for lack of counsel,
but with many advisers they succeed.

PROVERBS 15:22

You will have success if you are careful to observe
the decrees and laws that the LORD gave Moses for
Israel. Be strong and courageous. Do not be afraid
or discouraged.

1 CHRONICLES 22:13

Blessed are those who fear the LORD,
who find great delight in his commands.
Their children will be mighty in the land;
the generation of the upright will be blessed.
Wealth and riches are in their houses,
and their righteousness endures forever.

PSALM 112:1–3 TNIV

Success

May [God] give you the desire of your heart
and make all your plans succeed.
We will shout for joy when you are victorious
and will lift up our banners in the name of
our God.
May the LORD grant all your requests.

PSALM 20:4

The LORD said, "Do not let this Book of the Law depart from your mouth; meditate on it day and night, so that you may be careful to do everything written in it. Then you will be prosperous and successful. Have I not commanded you? Be strong and courageous. Do not be terrified; do not be discouraged, for the LORD your God will be with you wherever you go."

JOSHUA 1:8–9

Jehoshaphat said, "Have faith in the LORD your God and you will be upheld; have faith in his prophets and you will be successful."

2 CHRONICLES 20:20

There is no wisdom, no insight, no plan
that can succeed against the LORD.

PROVERBS 21:30

Success

The LORD was with Joseph and he prospered, and he lived in the house of his Egyptian master. When his master saw that the LORD was with him and that the LORD gave him success in everything he did, Joseph found favor in his eyes and became his attendant. Potiphar put him in charge of his household, and he entrusted to his care everything he owned. From the time he put him in charge of his household and of all that he owned, the LORD blessed the household of the Egyptian because of Joseph. The blessing of the LORD was on everything Potiphar had, both in the house and in the field.

GENESIS 39:2–5

Not that I have already obtained all this, or have already arrived at my goal, but I press on to take hold of that for which Christ Jesus took hold of me. Brothers and sisters, I do not consider myself yet to have taken hold of it. But one thing I do: Forgetting what is behind and straining toward what is ahead, I press on toward the goal to win the prize for which God has called me heavenward in Christ Jesus.

PHILIPPIANS 3:12–14 TNIV

Success

[The LORD] holds victory in store for the upright,
  he is a shield to those whose walk is blameless,
for he guards the course of the just
  and protects the way of his faithful ones.

PROVERBS 2:7–8

For lack of guidance a nation falls,
  but many advisers make victory sure.

PROVERBS 11:14

The horse is made ready for the day of battle,
  but victory rests with the LORD.

PROVERBS 21:31

For waging war you need guidance,
  and for victory many advisers.

PROVERBS 24:6

When the righteous triumph, there is great elation.

PROVERBS 28:12

Success

The sting of death is sin, and the power of sin is the
law. But thanks be to God! He gives us the victory
through our Lord Jesus Christ.

1 CORINTHIANS 15:56–57

Everyone born of God overcomes the world. This is
the victory that has overcome the world, even
our faith.

1 JOHN 5:4

The LORD has delivered me from all my troubles,
and my eyes have looked in triumph on my foes.

PSALM 54:7

[The LORD] is with me; he is my helper.
I will look in triumph on my enemies.

PSALM 118:7

Thanks be to God, who always leads us in triumphal
procession in Christ and through us spreads everywhere the fragrance of the knowledge of him.

2 CORINTHIANS 2:14

Success

We make it our goal to please him, whether we are at home in the body or away from it.

2 CORINTHIANS 5:9

Though you have not seen him, you love him; and even though you do not see him now, you believe in him and are filled with an inexpressible and glorious joy, for you are receiving the goal of your faith, the salvation of your souls.

1 PETER 1:8–9

The LORD declares,
"So is my word that goes out from my mouth:
It will not return to me empty,
but will accomplish what I desire
and achieve the purpose for which I sent it."

ISAIAH 55:11

Moses said, "Do not be afraid. Stand firm and you will see the deliverance the LORD will bring you today. The Egyptians you see today you will never see again. The LORD will fight for you; you need only to be still."

EXODUS 14:13–14

Temptation

Jesus said, "Watch and pray so that you will not fall into temptation. The spirit is willing, but the body is weak."

MARK 14:38

When tempted, no one should say, "God is tempting me." For God cannot be tempted by evil, nor does he tempt anyone.

JAMES 1:13

We do not have a high priest who is unable to sympathize with our weaknesses, but we have one who has been tempted in every way, just as we are—yet was without sin.

HEBREWS 4:15

People who want to get rich fall into temptation and a trap and into many foolish and harmful desires that plunge men into ruin and destruction. For the love of money is a root of all kinds of evil. Some people, eager for money, have wandered from the faith and pierced themselves with many griefs.

1 TIMOTHY 6:9–10

Temptation

If someone is caught in a sin, you who live by the Spirit should restore that person gently. But watch yourselves, or you also may be tempted.

GALATIANS 6:1 TNIV

Because [Jesus] himself suffered when he was tempted, he is able to help those who are being tempted.

HEBREWS 2:18

The sinful nature desires what is contrary to the Spirit, and the Spirit what is contrary to the sinful nature. They are in conflict with each other, so that you do not do what you want.... Those who belong to Christ Jesus have crucified the sinful nature with its passions and desires.

GALATIANS 5:17, 24

Sin shall not be your master, because you are not under law, but under grace.

ROMANS 6:14

Temptation

If you think you are standing firm, be careful that you don't fall! No temptation has seized you except what is common to man. And God is faithful; he will not let you be tempted beyond what you can bear. But when you are tempted, he will also provide a way out so that you can stand up under it.

1 CORINTHIANS 10:12–13

Put on the full armor of God so that you can take your stand against the devil's schemes. For our struggle is not against flesh and blood, but against the rulers, against the authorities, against the powers of this dark world and against the spiritual forces of evil in the heavenly realms.... Stand firm then, with the belt of truth buckled around your waist, with the breastplate of righteousness in place, and with your feet fitted with the readiness that comes from the gospel of peace.... Take up the shield of faith, with which you can extinguish all the flaming arrows of the evil one. Take the helmet of salvation and the sword of the Spirit, which is the word of God.

EPHESIANS 6:11–17

Temptation

Those who walk righteously
  and speak what is right,
who reject gain from extortion
  and keep their hands from accepting bribes,
who stop their ears against plots of murder
  and shut their eyes against contemplating evil—
they are the ones who will dwell on the heights,
  whose refuge will be the mountain fortress.
Their bread will be supplied,
  and water will not fail them.

ISAIAH 33:15–16 TNIV

The fear of the LORD is a fountain of life,
  turning a person from the snares of death.

PROVERBS 14:27 TNIV

Those who lead the upright along an evil path
  will fall into their own trap,
  but the blameless will receive a good inheritance.

PROVERBS 28:10 TNIV

Temptation

Do not set foot on the path of the wicked
or walk in the way of evildoers.
Avoid it, do not travel on it;
turn from it and go on your way.

PROVERBS 4:14–15 TNIV

If sinners entice you,
do not give in to them.
Do not go along with them,
do not set foot on their paths;
for their feet rush into sin,
they are swift to shed blood.

PROVERBS 1:10, 15–16

The farmer sows the word. Some people are ... like seed sown among thorns, hear the word; but the worries of this life, the deceitfulness of wealth and the desires for other things come in and choke the word, making it unfruitful.

MARK 4:14–15, 18 TNIV

Temptation

Be careful that you do not forget the LORD your God, failing to observe his commands, his laws and his decrees that I am giving you this day. Otherwise, when you eat and are satisfied, when you build fine houses and settle down, and when your herds and flocks grow large and your silver and gold increase and all you have is multiplied, then your heart will become proud and you will forget the LORD your God, who brought you out of Egypt, out of the land of slavery.... You may say to yourself, "My power and the strength of my hands have produced this wealth for me." But remember the LORD your God, for it is he who gives you the ability to produce wealth, and so confirms his covenant, which he swore to your forefathers, as it is today.

DEUTERONOMY 8:11–14, 17–18

You must rid yourselves of all such things as these: anger, rage, malice, slander, and filthy language from your lips.... You have taken off your old self ... and have put on the new self, which is being renewed in ... the image of its Creator.

COLOSSIANS 3:8–10

Thankfulness

Give thanks to the LORD, call on his name;
  make known among the nations what he
    has done.
Sing to him, sing praise to him;
  tell of all his wonderful acts.

1 CHRONICLES 16:8–9

Whatever you do, whether in word or deed, do it all in the name of the Lord Jesus, giving thanks to God the Father through him.

COLOSSIANS 3:17

Since we are receiving a kingdom that cannot be shaken, let us be thankful, and so worship God acceptably with reverence and awe.

HEBREWS 12:28

Just as you received Christ Jesus as Lord, continue to live in him, rooted and built up in him, strengthened in the faith as you were taught, and overflowing with thankfulness.

COLOSSIANS 2:6–7

Thanks be to God! He gives us the victory through our Lord Jesus Christ.

1 CORINTHIANS 15:57

Thankfulness

Let them give thanks to the LORD for his
  unfailing love
  and his wonderful deeds for men,
for he satisfies the thirsty
  and fills the hungry with good things.

PSALM 107:8–9

Devote yourselves to prayer, being watchful
and thankful.

COLOSSIANS 4:2

Thanks be to God for his indescribable gift!

2 CORINTHIANS 9:15

I will praise God's name in song
  and glorify him with thanksgiving.

PSALM 69:30

Enter his gates with thanksgiving
  and his courts with praise;
  give thanks to him and praise his name.

PSALM 100:4

Thankfulness

The LORD says,
"Sacrifice thank offerings to God,
    fulfill your vows to the Most High,
and call upon me in the day of trouble;
    I will deliver you, and you will honor me."

PSALM 50:14–15

Give thanks in all circumstances, for this is God's
will for you in Christ Jesus.

1 THESSALONIANS 5:18

Let us come before him with thanksgiving
    and extol him with music and song.

PSALM 95:2

Sing to the LORD with thanksgiving;
    make music to our God on the harp.

PSALM 147:7

Everything God created is good, and nothing is to
be rejected if it is received with thanksgiving,
because it is consecrated by the word of God
and prayer.

1 TIMOTHY 4:4–5

Thankfulness

I urge, then, first of all, that requests, prayers, intercession and thanksgiving be made for everyone—for kings and all those in authority, that we may live peaceful and quiet lives in all godliness and holiness. This is good, and pleases God our Savior.

1 TIMOTHY 2:1–3

The LORD will surely comfort Zion
and will look with compassion on all her ruins;
he will make her deserts like Eden,
her wastelands like the garden of the LORD.
Joy and gladness will be found in her,
thanksgiving and the sound of singing.

ISAIAH 51:3

I am under vows to you, O God;
I will present my thank offerings to you.
For you have delivered me from death
and my feet from stumbling,
that I may walk before God
in the light of life.

PSALM 56:12–13

Thankfulness

I will sacrifice a thank offering to you
    and call on the name of the LORD.

PSALM 116:17

I thank and praise you, O God of my fathers:
    You have given me wisdom and power,
you have made known to me what we asked of you.

DANIEL 2:23

I thank my God every time I remember you.

PHILIPPIANS 1:3

I thank Christ Jesus our Lord, who has given me
strength, that he considered me faithful, appointing
me to his service.

1 TIMOTHY 1:12

I will give thanks to the LORD because of
        his righteousness
    and will sing praise to the name of the LORD
        Most High.

PSALM 7:17

Thankfulness

Sing and make music in your heart to the Lord, always giving thanks to God the Father for everything, in the name of our Lord Jesus Christ.

EPHESIANS 5:19–20

You turned my wailing into dancing;
*   you removed my sackcloth and clothed me*
*   with joy,*
that my heart may sing to you and not be silent.
*   O LORD my God, I will give you thanks forever.*

PSALM 30:11–12

I will give you thanks in the great assembly;
*   among throngs of people I will praise you.*

PSALM 35:18

Is not the cup of thanksgiving for which we give thanks a participation in the blood of Christ? And is not the bread that we break a participation in the body of Christ?

1 CORINTHIANS 10:16

Thanks be to God, who always leads us in triumphal procession in Christ and through us spreads everywhere the fragrance of the knowledge of him.

2 CORINTHIANS 2:14

Trials and Tribulations

The Lord knows how to rescue the godly from trials
and to hold the unrighteous for punishment on the
day of judgment.

2 PETER 2:9 TNIV

Blessed are those who persevere under trial,
because when they have stood the test, they will
receive the crown of life that God has promised to
those who love him.

JAMES 1:12 TNIV

Consider it pure joy, my brothers and sisters, whenever you face trials of many kinds, because you
know that the testing of your faith produces perseverance. Let perseverance finish its work so that you
may be mature and complete, not lacking anything.

JAMES 1:2-4 TNIV

Do not be surprised at the painful trial you are suffering, as though something strange were happening
to you. But rejoice that you participate in the sufferings of Christ, so that you may be overjoyed when
his glory is revealed. If you are insulted because of
the name of Christ, you are blessed, for the Spirit of
glory and of God rests on you.

1 PETER 4:12-14

Trials and Tribulations

When you are in distress and all these things have happened to you, then in later days you will return to the LORD your God and obey him. For the LORD your God is a merciful God; he will not abandon or destroy you or forget the covenant with your forefathers, which he confirmed to them by oath.

DEUTERONOMY 4:30–31

After you have suffered a little while, [the God of grace] will himself restore you and make you strong, firm, and steadfast.

1 PETER 5:10

I consider that our present sufferings are not worth comparing with the glory that will be revealed in us.

ROMANS 8:18

Among God's churches we boast about your perseverance and faith in all the persecutions and trials you are enduring. All this is evidence that God's judgment is right, and as a result you will be counted worthy of the kingdom of God, for which you are suffering. God is just: He will pay back trouble to those who trouble you and give relief to you who are troubled.

2 THESSALONIANS 1:4–7

Trials and Tribulations

In this you greatly rejoice, though now for a little while you may have had to suffer grief in all kinds of trials. These have come so that your faith — of greater worth than gold, which perishes even though refined by fire — may be proved genuine and may result in praise, glory and honor when Jesus Christ is revealed.

1 PETER 1:6–7

"Blessed are you when people insult you, persecute you and falsely say all kinds of evil against you because of me. Rejoice and be glad, because great is your reward in heaven, for in the same way they persecuted the prophets who were before you."

MATTHEW 5:11–12

We have this treasure in jars of clay to show that this all-surpassing power is from God and not from us. We are hard pressed on every side, but not crushed; perplexed, but not in despair; persecuted, but not abandoned; struck down, but not destroyed. We always carry around in our body the death of Jesus, so that the life of Jesus may also be revealed in our body.

2 CORINTHIANS 4:7–10

Trials and Tribulations

To keep me from becoming conceited because of these surpassingly great revelations, there was given me a thorn in my flesh, a messenger of Satan, to torment me. Three times I pleaded with the Lord to take it away from me. But he said to me, "My grace is sufficient for you, for my power is made perfect in weakness." Therefore I will boast all the more gladly about my weaknesses, so that Christ's power may rest on me. That is why, for Christ's sake, I delight in weaknesses, in insults, in hardships, in persecutions, in difficulties. For when I am weak, then I am strong.

2 CORINTHIANS 12:7–10

When we are cursed, we bless; when we are persecuted, we endure it; when we are slandered, we answer kindly.

1 CORINTHIANS 4:12–13

The righteous cry out, and the LORD hears them;
*   he delivers them from all their troubles.*
The LORD is close to the brokenhearted
*   and saves those who are crushed in spirit.*
A righteous man may have many troubles,
*   but the LORD delivers him from them all.*

PSALM 34:17–19

Trials and Tribulations

We do not lose heart. Though outwardly we are wasting away, yet inwardly we are being renewed day by day. For our light and momentary troubles are achieving for us an eternal glory that far outweighs them all. So we fix our eyes not on what is seen, but on what is unseen. For what is seen is temporary, but what is unseen is eternal.

2 CORINTHIANS 4:16–18

Everyone who wants to live a godly life in Christ Jesus will be persecuted, while evil men and impostors will go from bad to worse, deceiving and being deceived. But as for you, continue in what you have learned and have become convinced of, because you know those from whom you learned it.

2 TIMOTHY 3:12–14

I am greatly encouraged; in all our troubles my joy knows no bounds.

2 CORINTHIANS 7:4

This poor man called, and the LORD heard him;
he saved him out of all his troubles.

PSALM 34:6

Trials and Tribulations

Praise be to the God and Father of our Lord Jesus
Christ, the Father of compassion and the God of all
comfort, who comforts us in all our troubles, so that
we can comfort those in any trouble with the comfort we ourselves have received from God. For just
as the sufferings of Christ flow over into our lives, so
also through Christ our comfort overflows.

2 CORINTHIANS 1:3–5

As servants of God we commend ourselves in every
way: in great endurance; in troubles, hardships and
distresses; in beatings, imprisonments and riots; in
hard work, sleepless nights and hunger; in purity,
understanding, patience and kindness; in the Holy
Spirit and in sincere love; in truthful speech and
in the power of God; with weapons of righteousness
in the right hand and in the left; through glory and
dishonor, bad report and good report; genuine,
yet regarded as impostors; known, yet regarded as
unknown; dying, and yet we live on; beaten, and yet
not killed; sorrowful, yet always rejoicing; poor, yet
making many rich; having nothing, and yet possess-
ing everything.

2 CORINTHIANS 6:4–10

Victory

When the righteous triumph, there is great elation.

PROVERBS 28:12

Jesus said, "In this world you will have trouble. But take heart! I have overcome the world."

JOHN 16:33

Who shall separate us from the love of Christ? Shall trouble or hardship or persecution or famine or nakedness or danger or sword? As it is written:

"For your sake we face death all day long;
*   we are considered as sheep to be slaughtered."*

No, in all these things we are more than conquerors through him who loved us.

ROMANS 8:35–37

To you, O LORD, I lift up my soul;
*   in you I trust, O my God.*
Do not let me be put to shame,
*   nor let my enemies triumph over me.*

PSALM 25:1–2

Victory

I know that you are pleased with me,
for my enemy does not triumph over me.

PSALM 41:11

[The LORD] has delivered me from all my troubles,
and my eyes have looked in triumph on my foes.

PSALM 54:7

Good will come to those who are generous and
lend freely,
who conduct their affairs with justice.
Surely the righteous will never be shaken;
they will be remembered forever.
They will have no fear of bad news;
their hearts are steadfast, trusting in the LORD.
Their hearts are secure, they will have no fear;
in the end they will look in triumph on their foes.

PSALM 112:5–8 TNIV

Do not be overcome by evil, but overcome evil
with good.

ROMANS 12:21

Victory

The LORD will march out like a mighty man,
*   like a warrior he will stir up his zeal;*
with a shout he will raise the battle cry
*   and will triumph over his enemies.*

ISAIAH 42:13

Jesus said, "I saw Satan fall like lightning from
heaven. I have given you authority to trample on
snakes and scorpions and to overcome all the power
of the enemy; nothing will harm you."

LUKE 10:18–19

I am writing to you, young people,
*   because you have overcome the evil one.*
I write to you, dear children,
*   because you know the Father....*
I write to you, young people,
*   because you are strong,*
*   and the word of God lives in you,*
*   and you have overcome the evil one.*

1 JOHN 2:13–14 TNIV

The LORD is with me; he is my helper.
I will look in triumph on my enemies.

PSALM 118:7

Victory

Jesus said, "I tell you that you are Peter, and on this rock I will build my church, and the gates of Hades will not overcome it."

MATTHEW 16:18

Every spirit that does not acknowledge Jesus is not from God. This is the spirit of the antichrist, which you have heard is coming and even now is already in the world. You, dear children, are from God and have overcome them, because the one who is in you is greater than the one who is in the world.

1 JOHN 4:3–4

Everyone born of God overcomes the world. This is the victory that has overcome the world, even our faith. Who is it that overcomes the world? Only the one who believes that Jesus is the Son of God.

1 JOHN 5:4–5 TNIV

[Ten kings] will make war against the Lamb, but the Lamb will overcome them because he is Lord of lords and King of kings—and with him will be his called, chosen and faithful followers.

REVELATION 17:14

Victory

Jesus said, "To those who are victorious, I will give the right to sit with me on my throne, just as I was victorious and sat down with my Father on his throne."

REVELATION 3:21 TNIV

They triumphed over him
by the blood of the Lamb
and by the word of their testimony.

REVELATION 12:11 TNIV

I press on toward the goal to win the prize for which God has called me heavenward in Christ Jesus. All of us who are mature should take such a view of things.

PHILIPPIANS 3:14–15

In all these things we are more than conquerors through him who loved us.

ROMANS 8:37

The LORD your God is the one who goes with you to fight for you against your enemies to give you victory.

DEUTERONOMY 20:4

Victory

We have heard it with our ears, O God;
    our ancestors have told us
what you did in their days,
    in days long ago.
With your hand you drove out the nations
    and planted our ancestors;
you crushed the peoples
    and made our ancestors flourish.
It was not by their sword that they won the land,
    nor did their arm bring them victory;
it was your right hand, your arm,
    and the light of your face, for you loved them.

PSALM 44:1–3 TNIV

May he give you the desire of your heart
    and make all your plans succeed.
We will shout for joy when you are victorious
    and will lift up our banners in the name of
        our God.
May the LORD grant all your requests.

PSALM 20:4–5

Wisdom

Wisdom, like an inheritance, is a good thing
and benefits those who see the sun.
Wisdom is a shelter
as money is a shelter,
but the advantage of knowledge is this:
that wisdom preserves the life of its possessor.

ECCLESIASTES 7:11–12

The wisdom that comes from heaven is first of all
pure; then peace-loving, considerate, submissive,
full of mercy and good fruit, impartial and sincere.

JAMES 3:17

Do not forsake wisdom, and she will protect you;
love her, and she will watch over you.
Wisdom is supreme; therefore get wisdom.

PROVERBS 4:6–7

If any of you lacks wisdom, he should ask God, who
gives generously to all without finding fault, and it
will be given to him.

JAMES 1:5

Wisdom

I guide you in the way of wisdom
and lead you along straight paths.
When you walk, your steps will not be hampered;
when you run, you will not stumble.

PROVERBS 4:11–12

Wisdom is sweet to your soul;
if you find it, there is a future hope for you,
and your hope will not be cut off.

PROVERBS 24:14

Do not be wise in your own eyes;
fear the LORD and shun evil.
This will bring health to your body
and nourishment to your bones.

PROVERBS 3:7–8

The foolishness of God is wiser than human wisdom, and the weakness of God is stronger than human strength.

1 CORINTHIANS 1:25 TNIV

Wisdom

The fear of the LORD is the beginning of wisdom;
  all who follow his precepts have good
    understanding.
  To him belongs eternal praise.

PSALM 111:10

Your commands make me wiser than my enemies.

PSALM 119:98

Where then does wisdom come from?
  Where does understanding dwell?...
God understands the way to it
  and he alone knows where it dwells....
He said to the human race,
  "The fear of the Lord—that is wisdom,
  and to shun evil is understanding."

JOB 28:20, 23, 28 TNIV

To God belong wisdom and power;
  counsel and understanding are his.

JOB 12:13

Wisdom

The price of wisdom is beyond rubies.

JOB 28:18

If you accept my words
    and store up my commands within you,
turning your ear to wisdom
    and applying your heart to understanding,
and if you call out for insight
    and cry aloud for understanding,
and if you look for it as for silver
    and search for it as for hidden treasure,
then you will understand the fear of the LORD
    and find the knowledge of God.
For the LORD gives wisdom,
    and from his mouth come knowledge
        and understanding.

PROVERBS 2:1–6

How much better to get wisdom than gold,
    to choose understanding rather than silver!

PROVERBS 16:16

Wisdom

Blessed are those who find wisdom,
  those who gain understanding,
for she is more profitable than silver
  and yields better returns than gold.
She is more precious than rubies;
  nothing you desire can compare with her.
Long life is in her right hand;
  in her left hand are riches and honor.
Her ways are pleasant ways,
  and all her paths are peace.
She is a tree of life to those who take hold of her;
  those who hold her fast will be blessed.

PROVERBS 3:13–18 TNIV

The wise in heart accept commands.

PROVERBS 10:8

Those who get wisdom love their own lives;
  those who cherish understanding will
    soon prosper.

PROVERBS 19:8 TNIV

Wisdom

Does not wisdom call out?
Does not understanding raise her voice?...
Wisdom is more precious than rubies,
    and nothing you desire can compare with her.
I, wisdom, dwell together with prudence;
    I possess knowledge and discretion.

PROVERBS 8:1, 11–12

Oh, the depth of the riches of the wisdom an
knowledge of God!
    How unsearchable his judgments,
    and his paths beyond tracing out!

ROMANS 11:33

Wisdom is supreme; therefore get wisdom.
    Though it cost all you have, get understanding.
Esteem her, and she will exalt you;
    embrace her, and she will honor you.
She will set a garland of grace on your head
    and present you with a crown of splendor.

PROVERBS 4:7–9

Words

Those who guard their lips preserve their lives,
    but those who speak rashly will come to ruin.

PROVERBS 13:3 TNIV

The mouths of the righteous utter wisdom,
    and their tongues speak what is just.
The law of their God is in their hearts;
    their feet do not slip.

PSALM 37:30–31 TNIV

Sin is not ended by multiplying words,
    but the prudent hold their tongues.
The tongue of the righteous is choice silver,
    but the heart of the wicked is of little value.
The lips of the righteous nourish many,
    but fools die for lack of sense.

PROVERBS 10:19–21 TNIV

From the fruit of their lips people enjoy good things.

PROVERBS 13:2 TNIV

Words

*May the words of my mouth and the meditation of
my heart*
   be pleasing in your sight, [O LORD].

PSALM 19:14

*From the fruit of their mouths people's stomachs
are filled;*
   with the harvest of their lips they are satisfied.

PROVERBS 18:20 TNIV

Always be prepared to give an answer to everyone
who asks you to give the reason for the hope that you
have. But do this with gentleness and respect.

1 PETER 3:15

A gentle answer turns away wrath,
   but a harsh word stirs up anger.
The tongue of the wise commends knowledge.

PROVERBS 15:1–2

Speaking the truth in love, we will in all things grow
up into him who is the Head, that is, Christ.

EPHESIANS 4:15

Words

If you speak, you should do so as one who speaks
the very words of God.

1 PETER 4:11 TNIV

Set a guard over my mouth, O LORD;
keep watch over the door of my lips.

PSALM 141:3

The Sovereign LORD has given me an
instructed tongue,
to know the word that sustains the weary.

ISAIAH 50:4

We all stumble in many ways. Those who are never
at fault in what they say are perfect, able to keep
their whole body in check.

JAMES 3:2 TNIV

The hearts of the wise make their mouths prudent,
and their lips promote instruction.
Gracious words are a honeycomb,
sweet to the soul and healing to the bones.

PROVERBS 16:23–24 TNIV

Words

Let your conversation be always full of grace, seasoned with salt, so that you may know how to answer everyone.

COLOSSIANS 4:6

The tongue that brings healing is a tree of life.

PROVERBS 15:4

A word aptly spoken
*   is like apples of gold in settings of silver.*

PROVERBS 25:11

A person finds joy in giving an apt reply—
*   and how good is a timely word!*

PROVERBS 15:23 TNIV

May the words of my mouth and the meditation of
*   my heart*
*   be pleasing in your sight,*
*   O LORD, my Rock and my Redeemer.*

PSALM 19:14

Words

The words of the wicked lie in wait for blood,
but the speech of the upright rescues them.

PROVERBS 12:6

Don't let anyone look down on you because you
are young, but set an example for the believers in
speech, in life, in love, in faith and in purity.

1 TIMOTHY 4:12

One who loves a pure heart and who speaks
with grace
will have the king for a friend.

PROVERBS 22:11 TNIV

The words of the LORD are flawless,
like silver refined in a furnace of clay,
purified seven times.

PSALM 12:6

My tongue will speak of your righteousness
and of your praises all day long.

PSALM 35:28

Words

My tongue will tell of your righteous acts
    all day long,
for those who wanted to harm me
    have been put to shame and confusion.

PSALM 71:24

Reckless words pierce like a sword,
    but the tongue of the wise brings healing.

PROVERBS 12:18

Before a word is on my tongue
    you know it completely, O LORD.

PSALM 139:4

Those who have no sense deride their neighbors,
    but those who have understanding hold
        their tongues.

PROVERBS 11:12 TNIV

The tongue has the power of life and death,
    and those who love it will eat its fruit.

PROVERBS 18:21